WHY CAN'T I HIRE GOOD PEOPLE?

LESSONS ON HOW TO HIRE BETTER

BETH SMITH

INDIE BOOKS
INTERNATIONAL

ISBN-10: 1-941870-90-2
ISBN-13: 978-1-941870-90-7
Library of Congress Control Number: 2017937810

Designed by Joni McPherson, mcphersongraphics.com

INDIE BOOKS INTERNATIONAL, LLC
2424 VISTA WAY, SUITE 316
OCEANSIDE, CA 92054

www.indiebooksintl.com

FOR RANDY

Your belief in my ability never wavered, no matter how hard things got.

—

FOR KATY

You once asked me for the first signed copy of this book. What a gift you are to me.

—

FOR THE BOULDER POLICE DEPARTMENT
UNIVERSITY HILL TEAM 2000–2005

Thank you for your dedication to the safety of all Hill patrons and for changing the course of my life at the same time.

TABLE OF CONTENTS

FOREWORD

"No comment!" I yelled to the reporters standing outside my restaurant. They were investigating a Colorado football recruiting scandal and my unfortunate participation in it.

For six years, I owned a bar and restaurant in Boulder, home to the University of Colorado. One night, the manager I had hired to help me run my business let in two underage football players, who subsequently were accused of committing a crime. This incident, part of the university's 2002 football recruiting scandal, made national news.

Because this manager's actions violated underage drinking laws, I was in trouble with the Boulder Police Department. Then the Boulder Fire Department accused me of allowing overoccupancy that night in the restaurant. And then the Boulder Environmental Enforcement Police cited me for excessive noise. The money, time, and energy I spent cleaning up the mess were astronomical.

My bad hiring decision had compromised the safety of my employees *and* my business neighbors *and* the larger Boulder community. It left me distraught, questioning my competence to run my business. When a business owner has to face the unfavorable outcomes of a hiring decision, the resulting emotions can be raw and powerfully negative.

I have a degree in social work, and I believe myself to be a people person. To have made a hiring decision that so dramatically affected my business and my community was gut-wrenching. I knew there *had* to be a better way. What had I missed when I interviewed this person?

When I met with the police department, I asked one of the detectives, "What can I do to make sure this doesn't happen again?" He replied, "You need to learn how to hire better."

So obvious. And absolutely correct. It was just that simple—and just that hard.

That conversation prompted a series of phone calls to other business owners. "I need to learn how to hire better. Can you help me?"

The responses I heard reinforced a common theme:

- "I'm not sure either, Beth. I don't know how to hire good people. So, once you figure it out, I hope you'll let me know."

- "This has always been a problem for me, and I've been in business for twenty years. I've never figured it out."

- "Sorry, Beth, I don't even know where to send you to learn how to hire better, because I haven't found anything that works."

- "Hiring just is what it is, and you just have to deal with turnover."

- "I always go into a new hire thinking I have a 50/50 chance as to whether or not they'll work out."

This wake-up call shook me to the core of my being. I vowed to never, *ever* put myself or my livelihood at risk again because I had failed to properly screen a job candidate. I went in search of an absolute foolproof method for hiring people. This book is the culmination of that search.

I simply wanted answers. I read every book about hiring I could find. All of them suggest pretty much the same approach: They talk about how dramatically expensive a "mis-hire" is. They talk about how we get it wrong. They talk about what you can legally ask in an interview and what you can't. They talk about references and criminal background checks and the "perfect questions" to ask. Each book insists on its particular formula for filtering out the best candidates.

What these books rarely or barely cover is the interview process, its structure, and protocol. Their authors typically state, "There are plenty of other resources on interviewing, so we're not going to cover that in this book," or something to that effect. But I've never found a book that focuses wholly and completely on the interview and candidate selection process.

In my research, I also read business journals, white papers, and academic studies. I read best-practices manuals from dozens of industries. I took a workshop from the Boulder Chamber of Commerce on hiring and other HR topics. I asked friends and family members how they were hired. I asked my fellow business owners for their hiring techniques. The hodgepodge of answers, styles and philosophies of hiring made it clear that hiring and keeping good employees is more luck than skill, and that *a lot* of time is spent managing turnover, low employee morale, customer-service mishaps, product-quality issues, and other consequences of poor hiring techniques.

I discovered that interviewing job candidates is a largely misunderstood science. Most managers "wing it," because they haven't been taught how to conduct an effective interview.

Disillusioned and uncertain that a truly good model for successful interviewing existed, I took a bigger-picture view to ponder, "How can I save my restaurant by hiring better people?"

The question inspired me to develop a system of interviewing that reveals a candidate's motivations, talents, desires, and passions. *This* is the meaningful information that enables an employer to effectively discern the absolute best fit for the role, the mission, and the culture of the company.

Why does that matter?

Every boss/manager/executive deserves to have the very best employees working for them. Think about the impact on the world: When companies hire the right people, work environments are pleasurable, productive, and innovative, and mountains move.

In 2006, I got out of the restaurant business and started A-list Interviews. I now teach businesses how to conduct interviews so that they are hiring the right employees and propelling their businesses forward. I want all businesses to have access to this process.

This book presents my Response Analysis System (a trademark of A-list Interviews). As an outside hiring manager, I've conducted over 20,000 interviews using this system; 91 percent of the first fifty hires were still employed by my clients after twelve months. Some are still there after *six years.*

That's why I wrote this book.

INTRODUCTION

You Have to *Learn* How to Hire Better

Your current or past hiring misfires may be less dramatic than mine, but your business is likely facing the challenge of underperforming, disruptive, or otherwise ineffective employees. According to Peter Drucker, world-renowned business consultant, two-thirds of all hiring decisions are found to be a mistake within the first year. You're certainly not alone in dealing with that issue—or with these:

You wonder, "Why can't I hire good people?"

- You struggle to find that perfect long-term employee who has passion for the position.

- You're uncertain about what to listen for in an interview to ensure that you have all the information you need to make a good decision.

- You get bogged down by the number of resumes you receive for an open position.

- You're unable to respond to each applicant in a timely manner.

- It seems like you should be looking for something specific in the resumes you receive.

- You wonder, "Where are all the good employees?"

- You think, "I can't hire, I don't know how to hire, and I don't know what to do about it because I still have to hire."

I provide a solution for these issues and many others you may not have bumped up against yet. My unique *Response Analysis System* comprises techniques that will ramp up your hiring practice—namely, the interviewing process.

The *Response Analysis System*, simply put, is a structured method of listening to the exact words of the candidate to determine if he or she is the right fit. This sounds easy; however, it is actually more sophisticated than you realize.

CLIENT WISDOM

"I liked that I didn't have to say anything if I didn't want to. The process was all mapped out. Every candidate got a fair shot at succeeding or not succeeding."

— Steve Caldara, President, Caldara, Wunder, and Associates

For example, imagine you have asked this question in an interview:

"Tell us about your best boss."

The candidate replies, "She was really easy to work with."

What is the most important word in that answer?

With. (You were going to say "easy," weren't you?)

"With" reveals the perception the candidate had of the relationship with the boss. She did not say "easy to work *for.*" Employees do not work *with* the boss; Employees work *for* the boss.

The *Response Analysis System* is a way to listen to a candidate's words without filters, biases, or interpretations. You have to take at face value what candidates say. If you don't, you end up missing the underlying communication or trying to decide if they meant something else, and that's counterproductive to the point of an interview.

You are about to learn:

- Why the current interview process doesn't work and how to fix it

- Why we interview the way we interview

- The psychology of the interviewer versus the interviewee

- How to clarify your vision for a position

- How to create an ideal candidate list

- How to use a job description effectively

- How to write a compelling job ad that invites the best candidates

- How to screen and filter resumes and applications to determine fit

- The critical components of the first, second, and third interviews

- How to maximize a new hire's impact

Confusion, resignation, stress, doubt, and anxiety all accompany a poor hiring decision. I know this from my own experiences and that of my clients. Such an internal state typically produces these unconstructive managerial behaviors and attitudes:

- Hiding turnover rates because of embarrassment

- Failure to properly train new hires

- Lack of accountability

- Internal promotions without adequate clarity of expectations

- Suspicion about employee activities

Such managerial dysfunction then shows up in the workplace as lower employee morale, tense relationships between managers and staff, and reduced productivity. Ultimately, your company's viability is at risk.

My objective is that you, upon turning the final page of this book, will have new or renewed confidence in your ability to make good hiring decisions that have immediate and long-term benefits for your business.

A heads-up: Please know that the *Response Analysis System* requires a lot of work. It will not make the hiring process quicker or easier *in the beginning*, but it will be time wisely invested.

Managing bad hires, constantly staying on top of them, putting out their fires, is the real time (and money) wasted. You necessarily spend valuable time on every new hire; I want you to do it up-front in the interview process, not on the back end, micromanaging them.

CLIENT WISDOM

"I have a new appreciation for what does and doesn't matter. I thought I was making mistakes in recruiting, but I was actually making mistakes in interviewing."
— Matt Mendez, Founder and President, SpinFusion

It is time to revolutionize your interview process so that you find the right person the first time—every time.

BEST OF BETH'S BLOG

Do Not Hire Good People

The question that every client invariably will ask me when we begin to develop their interviewing process is, "Why can't I hire good people?"

My poor clients are often doing their full-time jobs and the full-time jobs of other employees. My clients are tired, burned out, and are starting to hate the work they do because they need good help and are feeling overwhelmed. One client confessed to me that he hated going into the office every day because his direct reports have put piles of work on his desk that ultimately belong on their own desks. And his question to me was, "Beth, why can't I hire good people?"

My answer? You don't need good people. You need good *employees.* There is a big difference.

Think of it this way: I consider myself a good person. I vote, I recycle, I save dogs, I take good care of my clients. I hold the doors open for people, and I honestly care about our planet. Like I said: a good person. But if you put me in front of a computer for fifty hours a week with a set of headphones doing internet research, I would lose my mind. I would become a lunatic with a road-rage problem. A good person, but a terrible employee, because I would be in the wrong job. I need to be with people—working with people, talking to people—or I am not happy or productive.

Hiring good employees means hiring people for the right job. Hiring good people and putting them in a job they hate makes them bad employees. My advice? Do not hire good people: hire good employees.

•••

CHAPTER 1

....

This is Not a Coffee Chat

I realized, in retrospect, that my disastrous restaurant manager had made a troubling comment in the interview that I'd missed because his other skill sets were strong. I asked this candidate what type of person he would hire if he were in charge. He said "I'd hire a woman." In retrospect, he didn't even sell himself for the job. He isn't a woman, and yet that is who he would hire. The comment is sexist and short-sighted, and I ignored it. That single hiring mistake cost me a fortune to clean up.

Fact: Whatever you missed or dismissed about a hire during the interview will be what you eventually fire that employee for.

How did I miss something that was so obvious? Because I treated my interviews like the majority of hiring managers do—like a coffee chat. This is one of the biggest misperceptions about the interview process. The best hiring managers today have recognized that they need to do something more formal and less conversational.

Most people, even HR personnel, don't interview frequently. However, we all have conversations with coworkers, family members, friends, and strangers in the checkout line—all the time. Chatting is natural and easy, a somewhat basic skill. Take a minute to consider what you're doing when you're just chatting with someone. You're likely discussing something pleasant, noncontroversial, or inconsequential. People naturally find common areas of interest to focus on; the subconscious urge to make the conversation smooth and interesting is hard-wired.

If you're in a tough spot with a recent (or not-so-recent) hire, don't let it get you down. A poor hiring decision has nothing to do with your ability to form good relationships. Interviewing is a process completely different from choosing a friend or partner. It entails unique and distinct motives and leverage that shape the dynamic between people in a hiring scenario. An interview is unlike any other interaction you encounter, personally or professionally.

CLIENT WISDOM

"Having this process in place is an enforcer: it changes your level of commitment to the process and to the candidate that you hire."

— Rick Taylor, President, Lefever Building Systems

Consider this scenario: Two professionals—let's call them Becky and Don—have been acquaintances for a while, regularly seeing each other at networking and community events. There, they chat about their industry's trends, what the big players are up to, and how the local business scene is evolving. They recognize their connection and respect each other's opinions.

Becky and Don decide to have coffee. At their meeting, they brainstorm how they can serve each other's business. The tone of the conversation is a mix of pleasant curiosity, professional respect, and sincere enthusiasm for possible collaboration. Becky and Don perceive each other as equals.

In a different scenario, we have Anita and Barney. Anita's company has an opening for a key staff position, and she's responsible for the hiring process. She sets up an interview with the applicants whose resumes display the most relevant keywords and industry experience (more on that in chapter 4). The networking conversation, with its business-casual tone, comes naturally to Anita, and is the style of conversation she predictably brings to the interview setting. She is relaxed, friendly and confident.

Barney, one of the job candidates, is scared, impatient, and worried. His life is in an uncomfortable transition period. This is not normal for him. He will tell Anita anything she wants to hear so that he can get this position. He's not lying; he's not even exaggerating. He's surviving. Barney's thinking, "I have a family to feed. I've got a mortgage to pay. I've got things I need to accomplish, and I'm out of work."

Anita is just having a conversation, while Barney is confronting what feels like a life-or-death situation.

Barney is in for the fight of his life. Anita is just having coffee.

As the hiring manager, Anita is in a hurry: "I need somebody in here now." She typically isn't thinking big-picture about her company's long-term interests, or about how the role she's hiring for can evolve to advance the company. On paper, Barney looks good. She asks him questions, the answers to which she subconsciously knows won't disqualify Barney. For example, "Did you have trouble finding us?" or "I notice on your resume that you have these skills. Tell me about them." She's still having coffee. Barney, on the other hand, is anxious because he needs a job. An interview is extremely unnerving for him.

This tension leads Anita to stop asking questions and start selling the job, because that makes Barney feel more at ease. Anita gets into her comfort zone, selling the job and company, and Barney just listens to her. He is a captive audience. This shift, which neither will notice, has just ruined their chances of having a great employer/employee relationship, because Anita is now taking care of Barney, when the objective should be that Barney, the employee, helps his potential future employer, Anita.

Another surprise will be when new-hire Barney turns out to be a different person than interviewee Barney. Once hired, he will no longer be nervous; he'll be relieved—and happy. He'll love his new job, and probably bring energy and talent that wasn't apparent in the interview. It'll seem like a good thing—and Anita may have gotten lucky—but as time moves on, Barney could ultimately not be the best fit for the role or the company's culture.

Anita focused more on hiring Barney than on screening him. The interview didn't fully address expectations—Anita's and Barney's—or accountabilities—Barney's to Anita and Anita's to Barney— or Barney's passions and motivations. This is how you get on national news. (And not in a good way.)

BEST OF BETH

"Hiring has nothing to do with judgment."

Hiring is Easy: Interviewing is Hard

The dynamic between an interviewer and a job candidate is clearly unlike any other dynamic between two people in our culture.

Given what the words "interviewing" and "hiring" mean, the process can be this simple: "Barney, would you like to come work for me?"

"Yes, Anita, I would."

"Okay. You're hired."

See? Hiring *is* easy.

Interviewing, when done correctly, is hard, because the preparation before and during the interviewing phase—

and, by that, I mean *multiple* interviews—requires you to rigorously investigate your rationale and vision for hiring someone at all (see Figure on page 23 for an overview of the Seven Steps to Finding Great Employees).

BEST OF BETH

"Do you want just a butt in the seat, or do you want an employee to take your business to the next level? That's the question you need to answer."

Here's the deal: Hiring typically occurs with an urgent mindset that says, "We just need someone in here to do the job,"
If that's the way you're feeling, hire a temp. If some task can't wait to be completed, employ a temporary staffing agency to find you a generalist or a niche-skills placement agency to find you an interim specialist. It's okay to give yourself this breathing room.

That said, a temp is just that—a temporary solution. Sure, sometimes you get the random temp-to-permanent good fit, but this is rare.

Optimize your hiring outcomes via an interview process that takes luck, surprise, and randomness out of the equation. For every open position, you'll consider what evolving, expanded impact you want the role to have on your company and how the new hire can advance the company's objectives. You'll need to redirect your attention from past misfires and disasters, from doubt and resignation, to the future, to possibility and success.

This is what distinguishes the *Response Analysis System:* critical, intentional pondering on the front end by the hiring manager (really, *all* the players in leadership positions) constructs the pathway that leads to the best hire available.

©Glasbergen
glasbergen.com

"I can offer you a great benefits package:
liberal use of the company bike, paid nap time,
free cootie insurance, and a pension at age ten."

What do I ideally want in a long-term hire? Which candidate do I select to interview whose resume indicates a promising fit? Will this candidate fit my managerial style, the job requirements, and the company's culture?

Chapters 2 and 3 address outlining the perfect role, the ideal job candidate, and the comprehensive job description. Chapters 4 through 6 present a detailed protocol for interviews: the first interview screens for interpersonal compatibility; the second interview addresses the technical aspects of the job, its duties and accountabilities; and the third interview assesses the candidate's passion for the position. The close includes a reminder to train your new recruits. A great hire and a solid training program leads to less management (and turnover) overall.

A-LIST INTERVIEWS: 7 STEPS TO FINDING GREAT EMPLOYEES

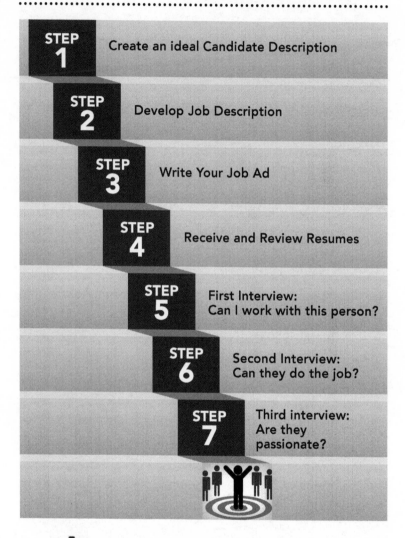

STEP 1 Create an ideal Candidate Description

STEP 2 Develop Job Description

STEP 3 Write Your Job Ad

STEP 4 Receive and Review Resumes

STEP 5 First Interview:
Can I work with this person?

STEP 6 Second Interview:
Can they do the job?

STEP 7 Third interview:
Are they
passionate?

A-list Interviews
find the right person the first time

CLIENT WISDOM

"I'd never written a job description before. I just sat down and hired."
— Lisa Haas, Founder and President, Actuate Social

"This exercise opened up pathways that were there but not visible. It took a stale process and added light to it."
— Rick Taylor, President, Lefever Building Systems

"It forces you to make sure that you educate the candidate on the job; then I can go back to that document for training and reviews. It levels the playing field for all parties."
— Janelle Lind, co-owner, Illuminations by Design

"It was the first time that we ever really thought about what we wanted."
— Roger Crawford, President, MEP Engineering

"This is an employee's road map to be successful in the job. You need to make sure that they can meet your expectations!"
— Anonymous

"It made me be intentional. I looked at that list every day."
— Dan Schachtner, Denver Station Owner, XPO Logistics-Global Forwarding

BEST OF BETH'S BLOG

You Are a Badass!

This is the title of the latest book that I have read by Jen Sincero, and every time I read it, pick it up or look at it, I think of you.

I know that right now you are struggling to find the best employees that you can possibly find and it is hard work. Slogging through resumes, interviewing candidates, trying to find the time to do your own job on top of that, and pulling your hair out at the difficulty of the process. After a really bad day of interviewing (or more than one) you wonder, "Where are all the good people?" You really want to give up and just hire someone already.

I want you to keep your chin up, because you are a badass. You deserve to have the best of the best, and those people are coming. Get in touch with how *amazing* it is going to be when these people finally get here. When they do, hang onto your hat; you will be floored at the difference they make, and you will be thankful that you held your ground and didn't give in to the temptation to just fill an empty chair with whomever.

In the meantime, when you have a lousy day, look back at how far you have come. Look at the changes that you have already made and what a difference it has made on your organization and your life.

Keep rocking it, you badass, you!

....

CHAPTER 2

What Are You Hiring For?

Step 1: Create an Ideal Candidate Description

Ask: *If I Could Have Anybody I Want for this Position, Who Would it Be and What Would He or She Know?*

I had this client who wanted to hire a CPA for his firm, and he kept saying to me, "If I could just hire someone... *anyone!*"

"But you *did* just hire 'anyone,' and you fired that person after two months," I argued.

We were both incredibly frustrated about the whole situation. That night, I woke up in a cold sweat at 3:00 a.m., and I realized that I had no idea what type of employee he wanted. I thought, "How on earth can I help him find what he wants if I don't even know what that is?"

The next day, I went to his office and I asked him this question: "If you could have whoever you wanted for this position, who would they be and what would they know?"

Below is the list we created together:

- Self-starter
- Knowledgeable
- Sense of humor
- Timely
- Conscientious
- Customer service skills
- Verbal and written communication skills
- Attention to detail
- Passionate about teaching
- Open to change
- Uses technology to create and support efficiency
- Time management
- People management
- Project management
- Deadline-driven
- Proposes new ideas
- Thinks in 3D: for example, how does the program think?
- Experience dealing with IRS preferred

- Technology: C.P.A. certificate, QuickBooks, Peachtree, Microsoft Office, typing skills and 10-key by touch

If you notice, there are very few skills listed here. Most of the list consists of attributes. He was able to envision his ideal candidate, and we were able to hire him an amazing employee.

The vision for a position is just like the vision for business. If you don't know where you are going and what you want from a business/employee, then you won't get anywhere.

One time I was interviewing for a client and the very first word on their ideal list was "focused." We interviewed a woman who, in the middle of a sentence, shoved her chair into a spin. As the chair spun around furiously, she threw her hands up in the air and shouted, "whee!" Does she seem focused to you?

About a year after this interaction, I taught a workshop with about twenty businesses represented in it. I divided them into groups and told them to come up with their "ideal list". They all mentioned the same attributes. My comment to them was, "I don't know anything about your businesses, but it looks like you are all looking for the same person."

Now, every client I work with begins with this exercise. They print the list and post it in strategic places around their offices, so that when they want to bang their head against the wall, they can refocus on their vision of the best employee *ever.*

The root cause of poor hiring outcomes is a lack of clarity about the specific, long-term expectations of the role. Fifty percent of all new hires leave their job within six months for two primary reasons. They didn't know precisely what the position required when they accepted the job offer, and/or they never got trained—both symptomatic of the hiring process.

You may have to consciously prompt yourself to think big during this step, especially if you're in a crisis mode. A lot of people will start off with: "Oh, my gosh, the last hire I had was horrible! I just want people to show up on time. I want people who don't cheat. I want people who don't throw their coworkers under the bus." You may be in a place of irritation or even despair about having to go through a hiring effort yet again. It is critical to release your past poor hires.

A danger in hiring when you are distraught because of a previous bad hiring decision is that, most likely, the experience dramatically affected the culture of your business, your numbers, and your success. Sometimes a bad hire can be traumatic enough that it affects your belief in your ability to run the company you've built.

Whether you're struggling with a troubled atmosphere or managing a more straightforward hiring scenario, it is always easier to ponder what you *don't* want. I want you to turn these ideas around and come from a positive perspective. This part can be both daunting and invigorating. You must take the time to envision the best attributes of an employee in the role you're hiring. You will use your most profound—and pragmatic—imagination.

"Well, I want my employee to show up on time, and to answer the phone when it rings. And I want…"

Let's just presume you have all that. You've gotten candidates to apply who have the basic skills. Go bigger. You can have whoever you want; dream big.

One client said: "Before, I was just looking to solve a problem, and now I want to look at creating a vision." This is a totally different mindset. You need to look at the big picture of where you want to go and what you want to accomplish.

Why is this important? Because one person on your staff can

CLIENT WISDOM

"Creating the Ideal List was a nice opportunity to come to a shared vision of what we were looking for. Also, because we were interviewing as a team, we had a chance to resolve any differences we had about that vision."

— Lisa Harris, 23-year marketing veteran

dramatically change the culture for either good or bad.
Think about a bully or someone who is abusive and how
dramatically they can ruin a company. Now think about the
flip side; you have someone who is perfect for a position
and they know it. They're happy when they walk in and
they do amazing work. It's really hard not to be inspired by
someone who is happy at work. That's what you want to
describe. That's the beacon that we're trying to create.

A lot of the descriptor words you should consider are
geared toward finding people who will work well with your
team: *motivated, reliable, energetic,* etc.

Additionally, when you have articulated the details of this
best-case employee, you can draw on that for inspiration
if the hiring process seems to be taking too long. When I
map out the *Response Analysis System,* many people think,
"That's just too much!" and get frustrated with the time it
takes to interview well. I tell them, "Go back to your ideal
list. Look again at the vision for this position, the ideal for
this position, and get tapped back into that *wow-ness* factor
of what it will be like when the person comes on board."

Once the vision of the perfect candidate has been
brainstormed, you need to keep this information on the
top of your mind. Do what my clients do: print it out and
strategically place it in a couple different areas around your
office and home. Hang one in your bathroom mirror, put

one in your car, one on your office; place it wherever it is that you will see it and start your mind generating energy around this ideal candidate.

One client confessed to me, "This step made me look at the person that I wanted, not the skill set. It is uncomfortable at first." Trust me; this hard work is part of what makes the *Response Analysis System* effective.

Step 2: Develop the Job Description

Ask: *What Will This Employee Do, What Will He or She Deliver, and How Should He or She Affect My Business's Key Goals?*

"Why, oh why do I have to write a job description?" my client whined at me. All of my clients complain about writing a job description, because it is hard and time consuming and boring.

"Because I said so."

And also, "Because you can't tell people what the job is if you don't *know* what the job is."

With this step, you will identify

> ## CLIENT WISDOM
> ....
>
> *"The Response Analysis System helped me define what I wanted. I had a picture in my head, but I saw things I hadn't seen before. I was sure one woman was a fit for the job. She wasn't."*
>
> — Eric Burkgren, Branch Manager, Academy Mortgage

specific tasks that will be accomplished by your new employee. Be thorough, as this same document can be used to map out your training program (More on that in chapter 8).

If you are not sure of all of the responsibilities and duties your new employee will be handling, ask team members, supervisors, and even exiting employees about the duties associated with the position you are filling.

Keys to a Powerful Job Description

1. **Set the parameters around the job.**

   Clearly describe the basic functions and the crucial skills necessary. List duties exactly; these are not attribute-based. You must write this in a way that is very clear and articulate so that the applicants know exactly what you expect of them. There are times that we will put a line in the job description saying a new hire must have X, Y and Z skills or formal training. For example, sometimes a CPA is required; you can't get around that certification. However, this sort of detail is something we use in the job ad, not the job description. (More on that in Step 3.)

The job description is really for you to get organized about who is going to do what—how does this role fit in with our current activities and our mission? You'll outline the activities this role will pursue on day one and throughout their tenure. This will provide the new employee with context as to how he or she fit into the big picture, as well as an idea of what he or she will be working on immediately.

There are other parameters that the job description will cover that come into play: let's say you're hiring a marketing director, and the marketing director has five direct reports. Go a step further and define those direct report positions as well to uncover any unmet needs. For example, if the marketing director is not going to be the one that does social media, who is? This process allows you to reframe your company, department hierarchy or reporting mechanisms depending on the job duties and goals. In fact, one job description allows you to look at an entire department and the company as a whole to reevaluate the effectiveness of the structure.

BEST OF BETH'S BLOG

Warm, Gooey Chocolate Chip Cookies

My daughter, Katy, and I love to make cookies, especially when it's snowing outside. We have a particular process: Melt the butter; sneak a few chocolate chips. Add the sugar and eggs; sneak a few chocolate chips. Add vanilla, baking soda, flour, etc.; sneak a few chocolate chips. Stir it all together; taste the dough. Sing to the song on the radio; dance; drop rounded tablespoons of the dough on the baking sheet; put the baking sheet in the oven. Dance a little more; taste another pinch of dough until the first batch comes out of the oven; eat a cookie while it's hot. Let it melt on your hand and chin. Giggle; pour a glass of milk, feeling a tad sick. We make cookies and memories all in one day.

One time, however, we put baking powder in the dough instead of baking soda and it was a disaster! Another time, we forgot the eggs; yet another time, we pulled the cookies out of the oven too late and they were burned. If you miss a necessary step in baking, you will ruin the final cookie outcome. The experience is the same when you are trying to hire the right person. There is a recipe for finding the right fit called the **Seven Steps to Finding**

Great Employees:

1. Create your ideal candidate in your mind
2. Write the job description
3. Write the job ad
4. Review resumes and schedule candidates
5. Conduct the first interview
6. Conduct the second interview
7. Conduct the third interview

When you miss one of these steps, it is like you burned your beloved chocolate chip cookies: gut wrenching!

Cultivating your staff begins with hiring the best, and you can't do that if you leave out a part of the recipe. So, pay attention, focus, and be patient when hiring your next employee. Also, don't forget to wipe the chocolate off your chin.

••

The job description is used for a homework assignment.

In the *Response Analysis System*, you're going to send candidates a full job description before the second interview, and you're going to have them read over it and come with questions. Most people have never read their job description. If one exists, they've never read it. This detail prompts buy-in for candidates; it allows them to more fully envision their role and daily activities. It also helps eliminate people who don't want to do the job. Once a woman came to a second interview with half of the job description highlighted in pink. She said, "The items highlighted in pink are the things that I will *not* be doing for you." Excellent. We now knew she wasn't a good fit.

2. **The job description is an anchor for employees regarding their deliverables.**

   You can't expect an employee to do something if it's not written down. One of the frustrations that I hear from candidates all the time is that they have a boss who threw them to the wolves when they had no idea of what they were supposed to be doing. They were never trained on what they were supposed to do and they left the position after having a miserable experience. With a proper job description, you can get buy-in for the job before the candidate is even hired for the position.

EMPLOYMENT AGENCY

"They're looking for someone who's well rounded and knows how to keep a cool head."

By the way, nobody ever wants to write job descriptions, often because people don't use them past the hiring date. In chapter 8, you will learn to buck this trend and find them valuable, much to your competitors' chagrin.

3. The job description guides future performance reviews.

So, after ninety days, after six months, after a year, you whip out this document. Is the job still the same? Many times, it is not. You can negotiate how that's going to work on the front end with the candidate, or later with your employee. This job description provides a very clear baseline from which to determine how well and in alignment the employee is doing their job.

An employee can use it to ask, "How am I doing?" And as the boss you can say, "Oh, you're doing great. You're doing this, this, and this. We're very satisfied," or say, "You know what? This description is no longer valid because of a variety of different reasons, and we would like to change such and such. How do you feel about that?" It's an active document that provides room for negotiation in the future regarding performance metrics.

4. **It helps fill the gaps.**
As the hiring manager, you have job duties that you are responsible for that must get done. Creating a solid job description helps you to determine who will do what. For example, if your Human Resources Manager isn't in charge of benefits, then who is? With robust job

CLIENT WISDOM

"This difficult, pick-and-shovel work was necessary to get the environment in my office that I wanted."

— Steve Caldara, President, Caldara, Wunder, and Associates

descriptions, you can map out who is responsible across the organization for all the activities necessary to implement the company's mission.

5. **Training:** One of the biggest complaints I hear from candidates is that they never received training. With a detailed task list, you can easily train your new employee. With intentional training, you get an employee who begins contributing to your organization immediately. It is a win/win.

You've taken two important steps in designing the foundation of the *Response Analysis System.* Now you're ready to move into the outreach phase and announce to the world, "This is the candidate I want!"

BEST OF BETH

"I have yet to go into a company that has a job description everybody is inspired and excited by— either it's gathering dust in somebody's file cabinet, or they don't have one at all. Existing ones are never accurate and usually haven't been looked at in a long time. Job descriptions are the last thing people want to spend time on, and yet they're a crucial part of framing the success and impact of your staff."

CLIENT WISDOM

"I thought a job ad was a laundry list of things I want this person to do. Through Beth's seven-step process, I learned that the job ad is about attracting the person I want."

— Lisa Haas, Founder and President, Actuate Social

"The Response Analysis System is clear, concise, basic, and simple. It works."

— Eric Burkgren, Branch Manager, Academy Mortgage

"Employees come in knowing exactly what to expect. We would say things in the ad like 'We want someone who isn't lazy,' and we would get lazy. Now we say, 'We want someone motivated to learn,' and we get people who are motivated to learn."

— Coralyn Wall, co-owner, Gonstead Family Chiropractic

"What I learned most is to be very clear in the ad. If the applicant wants another job than the one that I am offering, it is a waste of their time and mine."

— Jim Eddy, co-owner, Dream Dinners

"This is your invitation. It weeds out those who just want a job. I want the person who has done their research, and wants this job."

— Sean Lind, co-owner, Illuminations by Design

"The job ad is the intersection of how I see the position versus the marketing piece. It is an unusual space to be in to market a position."

— Rick Taylor, President, Lefever Building Systems

CHAPTER 3

....

Hiring = Marketing! The Job Ad

I am an interviewing nerd. I am *that* person who reads job
ads at 5:00 a.m., because I am fascinated by what people
write in them. I have read job ads online that put me right
back to sleep, and I didn't even apply for the job. I have
read ads that made me completely depressed afterwards.
One woman in Boulder, Colorado, posted a job for a nanny,
and her final line in the ad said, "If you are one of *those*
nannies from New York who thinks that you are going to
come in my house, make $15.00 an hour and do nothing,
you had *better* not apply!" Wow. That's encouraging.

Most companies skip writing an ad and just put the full
three-page job description online. It's not only boring, but it
is daunting, and there isn't anything that excites candidates
about the job.

When posting a job ad, you aren't simply putting out a
keyword-rich document searching for a composite of
skills walking around in a body. You're inviting someone
to consider joining your team if there's an appropriate
match—an alignment of vision, interest, and passion. You
begin with the mission: "Here's where we're going." You

begin with the big "Why We Do What We Do." This is vital to attracting the best candidates. Your screening process *starts* here. Those who don't agree with your mission need not apply.

Many jobseekers—especially since 9/11, it seems—want their work to mean something. They want to be a part of something larger than themselves. When they find the right fit, they demonstrate an intangible drive and energy to succeed. These are the "right people" you want to find through your interview process.

Recognize that advertising for a position is a *huge* opportunity to market your company. Each touchpoint with a candidate is a chance to show your vision, your culture, and your style.

For many candidates, this may be their first contact with you. Do not underestimate how valuable the interaction

CANDIDATE FEEDBACK

"I must tell you how impressed I was with the hiring process. I had been on several interviews in the past few weeks, and by far, the process with [this company] was the most professional and streamlined. Very impressive and refreshing! I always knew what was expected of me at each interview and knew what to expect following each meeting."

— Mary Barros, candidate of A-list Interviews client

can be in creating a positive impression. Imagine having unsuccessful candidates walk away with the thought, "Even though I didn't get the job, this seems like a great company. They treated me professionally and really have their act together."

Step 3: Write Your Job Ad

Ask: *What Is Our Mission, And Who Would Be the Best Fit? (Then Describe Them)*

Many people use the job description as the job ad; this is not the best way to entice the best candidates to apply. Use your ideal candidate exercise to create an exciting job ad that will pique interest with the workforce you desire to attract. You want to cast a wide net.

So how do you write a job ad that stands out? Here are a few tips:

1. **Use your mission statement in the first line of the ad.** Candidates want to know that their work is playing a part in something larger than themselves. They want to know that their work matters, so tell them *why* your company is doing what it does.

2. **Keep your ad short.** Begin with your mission statement, use a few bullet points to tell candidates what you are looking for, and then give clear instructions on how to apply. You can always give

candidates more information as the interview process continues.

3. **Do not use your job description as your job ad.** Usually job descriptions are long and tedious to read, so candidates will not spend the time to read them fully and completely. They will scan an ad, and you have three seconds to capture their interest.

In your ad, it is much better to have bullet points; they are much easier to read and translate into clear activities and deliverables, all within the context of the mission which has been articulated.

> ## THE BEST OF BETH
>
> *"Begin with your mission statement when writing an ad. After all, isn't that why you are in business?"*

"But wait," you say. "I just spent all this time working on the job description. It rocks! Plus, I don't feel like writing anything else, Beth…"

There are good reasons you don't want to simply repost your full job description as your job ad. First off, some people start reading through a three-page job description online, get intimidated, and start to feel like, "Gosh, I don't even know if I have all of those requirements."

If they aren't daunted by the details, they're skimming over them. Candidates scan job ads sitting in their pajamas with their fuzzy bunny slippers on Sunday morning as they cruise Craigslist, Indeed.com, or other online job portals. They aren't reading line-by-line, no matter what you think "good" candidates do. They're applying for 100 positions. They didn't read every bullet point. They scanned. So, provide them an ad that is easy to scan.

Another reason to create an ad focused on company mission and a few duties is that with a regular, full job description, you're posting proprietary information on the internet. Competitors don't need access to your detailed duties of the marketing director or technology officer or any other role.

Now there are often good reasons to list specific skills and formal certifications or experience requirements. For example, if you see a distinct advantage to hiring someone with an advanced degree in a certain industry, put that in the job description and then screen for that. If specialized licenses are required, such as for jobs that involve operating machinery, absolutely put that in your ad. You may choose to put in ads, "You must have a clean driving record," or that you're a nonsmoking environment, or other references to your culture and protocols. If you have certain policies for the workforce, you should mention those. For example, "We are a drug-free environment and require an applicant to pass a pre-employment drug screening."

This process helps screen out whether an applicant wants *this* job or simply *a* job.

More importantly, you want to be crystal clear about what type of person is a great fit and create energy for the position via the mission statement. People will not select a job as off-handedly if the mission doesn't resonate.

For example, one company mission statement is, "To enchant our customers and our vendors." Their outlook is, "We live in the world of enchantment. It's magical. We want our clients to have a magical experience." It's a beautiful mission statement. When you read that, you immediately have a sense of the culture and atmosphere at this company.

CANDIDATE FEEDBACK

"When I read the ad, I thought, 'That's me!' That is exactly what I do every day anyway!"

— Shauna Forde, recent candidate and hire

Then you say you're looking for a certain person to join your team. You put some inspirational bullet points into the ad—bullet points that focus on the big picture. A lot of the standards are:

- Someone who's a team player
- You show initiative

- You're passionate about this type of work

- You're passionate about serving our customers

- You love our culture

- You love this company

Another reason to focus on your job ad having a visionary and mission-oriented theme is to help stem the tide of half-hearted applicants, given the ease with which people can apply for employment online.

The dynamic of candidate and interviewer has really changed since the rise of Craigslist. I remember right out of college, I had to put on my pantyhose and my suit, with hard copies of my resume in hand, and I drove around to different companies. Hopefully I got to talk to somebody. Well, I could only afford to do ten of those in a day. Maybe.

But now, don't forget that your candidate can apply for 100 jobs sitting in yoga pants and t-shirt on a Sunday morning and be done before noon. Candidates of today throw pasta against the wall and they see what sticks. Before online applications, you might get fifty resumes for a job; now we're seeing 300, 500 or more.

Lastly, you list skills or certifications that are necessary for the position, such as experience with Salesforce, LinkedIn, etc. Microsoft Office Suite is a big one, or other computer skills, materials handling licenses, certifications, etc. You may list "years of experience," although that is a mixed bag (more on that in chapter 4).

The power of a great job invitation: This is reportedly a copy of an ad Ernest Shackleton placed to recruit for his 1915 Antarctic expedition.

Finding the People Who Believe What You Believe

(Excerpted from Simon Sinek's book *Start with Why*)

Early in the twentieth century, the English adventurer Ernest Shackleton set out to cross 1700 miles across Antarctica. His ship and crew would never reach the continent however; in the southern Atlantic their ship encountered mile after mile of pack ice, and was soon trapped as winter moved in early and with fury. Ice closed in around the ship "like an almond in a piece of toffee," a crew member wrote. Shackleton and his crew were stranded in the Antarctic for ten months as their ship—the aptly christened "Endurance" —drifted slowly north, until the pressure of the ice floes finally crushed the ship. On November 21, 1915, the crew watched as she sank in the frigid waters of the Weddell Sea. Stranded on the ice, the crew of the Endurance boarded their three lifeboats and landed on tiny Elephant Island. There Shackleton left behind all but five of his men and embarked on a hazardous journey across 800 miles of rough seas to find help. Which, eventually, they did.

What makes the story of the Endurance so remarkable, however, is not the expedition, it's that throughout the whole ordeal no one died, there were no stories of people eating others and no mutiny. This was not luck. This was because Shackleton hired good fits. He found the right men for the job. When you fill an organization with good fits, those who believe what you believe, success just happens.

Read more at Simon Sinek's website **www. StartWithWhy.com.**

Can They Read Directions?

Weeding Out the Bunny-Slippered Pasta-Throwers

At the bottom of our job ads, there's a list of directions. "If this sounds like the opportunity for you, please send 1) resume and 2) cover letter to 3) [client name]; 4) include the job title in the subject line or in the header of your cover letter." (Note: In order to follow ADA requirements, you must accept regular postal mail delivery for job applications; you cannot say "electronic/online/e-mail submissions only." Check with **www.ada.gov** for details.)

Put the job title in quotes in your ad, and at the bottom, end with, "We look forward to hearing from you." This is an invitation.

On the surface, those four pieces of information are necessary to put their application into the correct stream for analysis. This also shows whether or not someone is interested enough to follow those four directions correctly. *This is the very first screen: it shows whether people have at least a minimal level of interest in the job, sufficient enough that they can be focused and intentional enough to follow directions.* This is also indicative of their ability and willingness to follow directions in general.

We respond to every inquiry, assuming they did include a

contact address, phone number, or e-mail. If people cannot follow these four directions, they have already shown themselves to not be worthy of further attention. We then move our attention to the rest of the candidates who could follow the directions. Again, the *Response Analysis System* quickly reveals a shorter list of more worthy candidates.

You're moving now; the ideal candidate for your visionary role is getting closer. There is still a lot to do, however. Next, we're going to review those applicants who have made it through the first filter and choose who to interview.

BEST OF BETH'S BLOG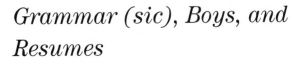

Grammar (sic), Boys, and Resumes

My daughter, Katy, received a text from a potential suitor that said, "Your so pretty!"

She showed me the text with a horrified look on her face and said, "I'm sorry. If he doesn't know the difference between your/you're and to/two/too, then I am not interested!"

In my business, we receive hundreds of resumes for jobs per week and at least half of them have some sort of grammar and/or spelling error. Sometimes we interview the applicants anyway because they have the experience that we are looking for, they wrote nice cover letters, or we decide to forgive that "one tiny mistake." But here is the hard-and-fast truth: The easiest way to determine if a candidate is serious about the position is whether he or she took the extra two minutes to run spell-check and proof his or her work. It really isn't hard. It really doesn't take much time. It really does make a difference.

So, for those candidates who are continuously asking me for interviewing help, my best advice to get the interview is to please do a review of your materials before you send them. Better yet, have your neighbor, friend, or significant other read your resume and cover letter, just for that extra set of eyes. And for my clients who ask: Yes! Grammar counts. Just ask my beloved teenage daughter.

P.S. May all boys within dating age of my daughter make grammatical errors like these. Amen.

....

CLIENT WISDOM

"I used to look for commonalties, like where they are from. Now, I look for character. It is so much better!"
— Coralyn Wall, co-owner of Gonstead Family Chiropractic

"It is easy to eliminate people who can't follow directions."
— Carol Eddy, co-owner of Dream Dinners

"Resumes tell you nothing about a person. You learn more from their cover letter than you ever do from the resume. Also, the instructions are very powerful— that is an interview in and of itself."
— Sean Lind, co-founder of Illuminations by Design

"It is interesting to see how candidates put their homework together- what slant they take. Several times we found out they weren't honest about their expertise."
— James May, Vice President for First Financial Bank (retired)

"What I learned is that the skill section just isn't important. I can teach skills, but I can't teach personality. In addition, I no longer worry about job hopping. People can job hop to look for the right fit, so I now give it less weight."
— Jim Eddy co-owner of Dream Dinners

"I realize the importance of responding to every candidate from a marketing perspective. I had never considered the candidate experience before."
— Lisa Haas, Owner, Actuate Social

CHAPTER 4

....

Reviewing Your Candidates

Once at my restaurant, I had a potential door staff employee come in and ask for an application to fill out. He then asked me if he could take it home and bring it back later. I said absolutely. He brought it back later, filled out, with handwriting that was obviously female. I looked down at the application, stared for a few seconds and looked up at him with a question in my eye. He looked down sheepishly and said, "My handwriting is terrible, and I wanted you to be able to read it. So, I asked my girlfriend to fill it out for me."

I am happy to say that I did conduct a formal interview with him, although I wanted to hire him on the spot, and he became one of my best employees.

So, then, the question became, how do I know who is a good fit by reading resumes?

You've built the foundation of the *Response Analysis System*. Now you have some on-the-court work ahead. You will read the resumes of all the applicants who followed your submission directions to the letter and filter them into the first of the three interviews.

Step 4: Receive and Review Resumes

Ask: *Did the Applicant Follow Directions? Does He or She Have the Minimum Skills?*

If the applicant fulfilled the preliminary information requests, first review the resume for nonnegotiable qualifications, like a particular license or certification, or specific training or education. Maybe you need someone who can develop software, or knows tax implications for a nonprofit, or speaks a certain language, or has a state permit to handle exotic animals.

Respond to every resume you received. It's marketing on behalf of your company to a current or prospective customer, and it's considerate and respectful. Your standard reply can be straightforward: "Thank you for your interest. There is not a match for your qualifications at this time." Or a little warmer: "We really appreciate your time, and we wish you the very best of luck in your future." How hard is that?

BEST OF BETH

"The biggest waste of time is spent trying to judge a person on a resume that the candidate most likely didn't write."

This may be the only time the applicant has contact with your company. Why miss the chance to treat them better than 99 percent of the other companies they will apply to, which are almost certain to leave them in the dark about their status in the hiring process? People are incredibly grateful when you communicate with them. It's not the rejection for a position, but the waiting to find out, that demeans applicants and saps their energy. Make that small effort to ensure that your company isn't seen as part of the difficult and impersonal part of a job search.

This next directive may sound daunting: you must interview 10 to 20 percent of your candidate pool if you want to optimize your final selection. If you receive a hundred resumes, you'll interview ten to twenty candidates (actually, if you had fifty applicants, I'd advise you to talk to ten to twenty of them).

"Whoa, what?" I can hear you say. To interview that many people efficiently, we shorten the first interview dramatically.

The first interview is only fifteen minutes.

And what you'll learn in these short interviews will inform your filtering process in ways you won't perceive at the time. The traditional hiring manager says, "I'm looking to filter on

CLIENT WISDOM
· ·

"This system makes all parties be intentional and clear; it is a self-elimination process that reveals the best candidate."

— Dan Schachtner, Denver Station Owner, XPO Logistics- Global Forwarding the front end. Just send me the top five candidates." The *Response Analysis System* doesn't do that. It filters on the back end and doesn't put too much stock in any one resume.

Three reasons to take resumes with a grain of salt:

1. Fifty percent of the information on resumes, in my experience, tends to be a lie or an exaggeration.

2. Someone may look great on paper, but the minute he or she walks through the door, you know instinctively it's not going to work. Plus, years of experience is problematic if what comes with it are years of bad habits.

3. Someone may not look great on paper, but can bring skills to the role that won't be revealed until you sit down and *listen* to him or her. Or you may value someone's excitement and passion over lack of experience and teach him or her how you want the job done.

So why are we spending all this time reading resumes when *at least half* the information is typically an embellishment or a flat-out lie? I asked a client once how much time he spent preparing for an interview with a salesperson. He read the resume and spent approximately fifteen minutes. "How much money does a good salesperson make for you?" I asked. He said, "Three million." I said, "So, you spend fifteen minutes preparing for a three million dollar deal?"

**"Loyalty and enthusiasm are the two things
I value most in an employee. You're hired!"**

Also, when we read a resume, we generally look for
experience and skills, which should not be the basis for
interviewing the first cut of applicants. Experience and
skill are only part of the picture of an ideal candidate. What
counts is whether they will be excited about the work
they're doing. Everything else can be gained and trained.

The most beautiful resume that I ever read brought a tear to
my eye. It was *awesome*. I decided right then and there that
I had found my person and that I was going to make a hiring
decision *that* day. The woman didn't like the interview,
saying that it was too short. She stood up and pounded her
fist on the table and screamed at the interview team, "*I am
not finished telling you about myself!*" We had to have her
escorted by security off the premises. After this experience,
I changed the way I reviewed resumes (meaning, I no
longer review resumes. I have my assistant do it).

When I facilitate interviews for my clients, I never read the resumes; I go into every interview blind, as do my clients. This way, we have no preconceived notion about the candidate when they walk through the door. None. We see only the candidate's first name and last initial. Any red flags, any skepticism about veracity, come not from the resume, but from across the table.

The Myth of the Top Five

"Just send me your top five people."

I want to debunk the idea that somehow there is a "Top Five" best candidate list for a position just waiting to be plucked from the pool of candidates for any given job.

Often, when companies work with recruiters, this is a common request. Hiring managers do not have the time to wade through dozens—or hundreds—of applications. Ah, if only finding the top five was that easy. Of course, the idea of a top-five most-qualified list of candidates is a major-league, over-the-top urban legend. Keyword scanning, the experience trap or some other coarse filter on the front end is no way to start your interview process.

First, when a recruiter selects five people to interview, he or she is not necessarily making the selections you would make. My Top Five people are not the same as your Top Five people.

©Glasbergen
glasbergen.com

"Instead of my résumé, I've printed out my daily
horoscope for the past year. You'll see that I'm a
special person who's destined for great things!"

Second, years of experience is often the top criteria for
eliminating and selecting candidates. Experience can be
a mixed-bag criteria on which to select candidates. I have
seen people with three years of experience who run circles
around people with twenty years of experience. I have
seen people with twenty years of experience who hate
their jobs. Many times, the experience listed on a resume
merely shows an ability to accomplish the job, without
any indication of desire, attitude, or work ethic when
performing the job. Rather than looking for people who
can do the job, look for people who *want* to do the job.
Open the door to people who are making career changes or
who may not have as much experience as you desire. Look
for the person who cannot wait to do this job. Experience
means very little and is often arbitrary.

Third, the idea behind a Top Five is that you can somehow cut to the chase of the "best" candidates and then schedule an hour-and-a-half interview with just those top five people. At this point in your hiring process, you will have spent seven or eight hours (in other words, all day) on five people. And you most likely will not have found the new employee you desire.

With the *Response Analysis System,* you will spend fifteen minutes with ten to twenty people and have an intentional first interaction that is critical when screening a passionate candidate pool.

Now you may say, "Beth, if I cannot screen resumes on keywords or experience, what is left?" The *Response Analysis System* screens for those candidates who are passionate about the job offering. What you look for when screening candidates is whether they followed the directions on the job ad explicitly. This attention to detail and completion is directly related to the passion for the job; the next step is to begin the actual interviewing.

BEST OF BETH'S BLOG

The Experience Trap

Every client I begin to work with wants a certain level of experience for the position they need to fill. They say, "Beth, the person needs to have five years of experience. Not negotiable." The problem with experience is that it is a mixed bag. According to the book *Talent is Overrated*, people with lots of experience were no better at their jobs than those with very little experience." Are you shocked? The book goes on to say, "Researchers from the INSEAD business school in France and the US Naval Postgraduate School call the phenomenon 'the experience trap'". Their key finding is that while companies typically value experienced managers, rigorous study shows that, on average, 'managers with experience did not produce high caliber results'".

So, if experience does not make for good hires, what does? Basically, you are looking for three traits in good people:

1. Can they handle conflict resolution? Whether there is conflict with the boss or conflict with a team member, how do these people resolve it? If your employees need you to solve their problems for them, then that is what you will spend your time doing. It is called management.

2. Can they do the job? This sounds like experience, right? It is not. It is more about basic communication and teamwork. Do they want to help the customer? Do they take ownership of their work? Do they ask for help when they need it? These are the qualities of employees who are self-sufficient and motivated to get the job done.

3. Do they want the job? Are they passionate about the work they do? If so, then they do not mind the occasional drudgery of the job. They love to solve the problems of the position and this motivates them to innovate.

If you want to hire good people, do not get caught in the experience trap. Find people who can solve conflict, have basic customer service skills and the passion for the job, then train, train, train. In the end, you will then have to manage less. You will be so glad that you did.

BEST OF BETH

"Hurrying through the interview process never works. Making a bad hiring decision just to put a 'butt in the seat' is always costlier than having a little patience to truly screen and interview. You will find your ideal new employee."

Why Three Interviews?

Speaking with your potential new hire three times gives you the ability to gain knowledge about a candidate's cultural fit, work ethic, management requirements, and more. The first interview is a quick check for basic fit, asking the questions, "Can I work with this person? Can he or she work for me?" The session is a fifteen-minute evaluation that reveals more than you may believe when you listen to word choice (more in chapter 5). The second interview (chapter 6) uncovers a candidate's skills, aptitude, and interest level. The third interview (chapter 7) reveals the candidate's deepest motivations and passion for the job (or not). Each interview is essential to gathering enough information about your candidate to make a knowledgeable choice, rather than relying on the "gut" feeling on which many hiring decisions are based.

Now get ready for a few power hours ahead—your fifteen-minute interviews with a range of candidates begins!

BEST OF BETH'S BLOG

Follow Your But, Not Your Gut

I just read yet another article talking about how hiring with your gut never works. As a matter of fact, hiring based on your gut reaction not only sets up your employees to fail, but also increases the risk you will hold on to them longer when you know they are not right for the positions, because your gut is involved. So, what exactly does all this mean?

If you have been around me long enough, you have heard me tell you that your gut does not help you in the interview process because the candidates are trying to sell to you. They want a job. They are anxious, worried, nervous, and scared. They *will* tell you what you want to hear, because they want a job. Remember: an interview is not a normal interaction, so the dynamics are off. Therefore, your gut reaction will be skewed and will not help in making a good hiring decision.

Instead, I want you to go with your "but." The "but" is the potential big problem, the proverbial "pebble in your shoe." You will talk about your potential employee like this: I like this and this about her, *but*...she doesn't seem to want the job. I really like *XYZ* about him, *but* he complained about the commute. If the *but* is something that you can live with and will not bug you later, then you can dismiss it from your hiring criteria. If you ignore it, you will make a bad hiring decision.

....

CLIENT WISDOM

"I am a good listener, and I took in so much information in just fifteen minutes! I was so tired afterwards!"

Eric Burkgren, Branch Manager, Academy Mortgage

"It is amazing how quickly people expose their red flags."

— Carol Eddy, co-owner, Dream Dinners

"It is really uncomfortable at first to limit interviews to fifteen minutes. But if you can stick to it, you can interview so many more people. Or, you can spend that time reading resumes."

— Dan Schachtner, Denver Station Owner, XPO Logistics-Global Forwarding

"I can't believe how much information I get out of a fifteen-minute interview. It's a time-saver on both ends—incredibly efficient."

— Lisa Haas, Founder and President, Actuate Social

"The 'shutting-up' part is really hard for me. You have to learn to be comfortable when they are uncomfortable. We don't need to impress the candidate—they are already interested in working for us, because they applied for the job. We need to spend time getting to know if they are the right fit for us."

— Jon Wall, co-owner, Gonstead Family Chiropractic

"You learn so much in the first interview. They either make it or break it. You can easily interview eight to ten people in a day. It's quick and easy, which is really nice."

— Janelle Lind, co-owner, Illuminations by Design

CHAPTER 5

••

Step Five: Can I Work with This Person?

When I began my journey to find out how to hire good
people for my restaurant, I had an infant daughter, a
husband, a restaurant to run, and oversaw two nonprofits.
To say that I had no time was a gross understatement. So,
I began with this question: Could I interview someone
in fifteen minutes and get all the information needed
to determine I could work with this person? After all,
restaurant environments require teamwork and often long
hours spent together. This became my signature "screening"
first interview. And, boy, is it accurate.

The first interview is designed to gauge the personality of
the candidate and cultural fit into your organization. This
session will be short and concise, with the goal of revealing
how the candidate may respond to stress, management
style, adversity, and conflict. The first interview is the same
for every position, from entry level to C-level.

The first interview, whether face-to-face or by phone, is
fast. Fifteen minutes. "How can that be worth it?" you
ask. I'll tell you how. This first interview will expose
whether the candidate is a brilliant technician on paper

but a horrible employee in practice. If you've conducted interviews, you know what I mean: People are late, disheveled, all manner of unprepared. Their demeanor shouts, "Hey, I don't know anything about your company. I have no idea what this job is." They've done no research and are really only interested in any job rather than *this* job. It's clear they are not a fit from the get-go. Grant them fifteen minutes, and then move on to people who want the position, who really want to be there. I have seen all the above plenty of times. It's a torturous waste of your time and energy to go through the motions of an hour-long interview with somebody that you could know within a few short minutes is not a fit. So, let's keep the first interview quick and simple.

If you listen to your candidate's words, you can also predict whether a person will bully the staff, be

> ### BEST OF BETH
>
> *"I've had C-level candidates come in to first interviews with documents printed all in green because the 'printer ran out of ink'—and this was a 1:00 p.m. midweek appointment. I had a guy who was drunk when he walked in. There was even one person who brought her mother to help answer questions. There are definitely people that you don't want to spend an hour-and-a-half with."*

inappropriate, or hand off his or her work to others. In fact, when interviewing, write down as much of the exact language used by the candidate when they answer your questions. We often write down what we think we heard or what we think a candidate meant. Instead, when you write down the exact words used, you can review the language after the fact which can provide insight into how the individual works. For example, a candidate once told me that his last boss was "a complete jerk with no redeeming qualities." If I wrote down that he said his last boss said bad things to him, I have downplayed the meaning of his statement and may miss something critical.

That One Question You Must Ask

I am certain you have heard that if you just ask the right questions, you will be able to find the perfect new employee. You've seen the book titles making such promises. It's a myth. You can ask one, three, or a thousand questions and still not get the information you need to make a good hiring decision. Questions serve to prompt the interviewee to the next topic or to expand on a previous response. And, yes, the questions relate to the information we are seeking, but a true interview allows the candidate to fully express himself, to reveal priorities, work style, and initial desire for the job. It's not about getting through a checklist of "perfect" questions.

A brief note on the rise of creative and stress-assessing interview questions that some prominent companies have become known for. Your candidates are already stressed. I believe it is borderline abusive to ask irrelevant questions like "How many golf balls fit in a 747?" Stress limits creativity; we should not be contriving additional stress within the first interview. Instead, ask intelligent questions and listen to responses.

While there are no magic questions to ask, there are a few that are used in the *Response Analysis System* so you can make a quick assessment for core requirements:

1.   What is your schedule? Include any vacations, possible start date and availability. (If interviewing an out-of-town candidate, also ask about potential relocation plans.)

2.   Tell me about the manager who inspired you.

3.   Tell me about the manager whom you never want to see again.

4.   Tell me about a time that you were overwhelmed and how you handled it.

5.   Tell me about a time when you helped a team member (someone of your equal rank.)

6.   Tell me about a time that you had a conflict with a team member and how you resolved it (equal rank).

7. What questions do you have for us?

Your candidates may be surprised that you're not asking questions related to the responsibilities of the position. Their reaction is the first observation to make. They are in a situation in which their expectations may differ from reality and they are not in a position of authority to alter that reality.

CLIENT WISDOM

"This shows you the person's character. You can tell if they want the job, how they deal with conflict, how they communicate with a team."

— Roger Crawdford, President, MEP Engineering

This alone will reveal their personality. Do they seem caught off-guard or confused? Or are they going with the flow, following your lead?

The first question determines schedule availability. Weed out quickly candidates who cannot take the job due to any logistical reasons. For example, one mid-September, a client and I were interviewing a woman who was going to be in Italy for the month of October, delaying her reasonable start date to the second week of November. We knew that was not going to work for us, as the increase in workload was scheduled to begin mid-October. We recommended that she contact us when she returned. If the position was not filled by then, we wanted to talk to her again. We ended up finding another candidate who could start sooner. Similarly, some people who do not want to relocate will apply for an out-of-the-area position, sometimes hoping they can telecommute. If your company is dead-set on having employees live locally to work on-site or attend in-person staff meetings, you'll want to nip in the bud a candidate's conflicting objectives to save time and energy for both of you.

CLIENT WISDOM

"The first thing I had to learn was that I'm not selling my business in an interview. I needed to talk less and listen more. Writing down everything they say allows you to go back and review."

— Jim Eddy, co-owner, Dream Dinners

Then as you continue to ask the additional questions, remember that one of the goals of the first interview is to determine how a candidate manages stress and conflict. We want to understand behaviors when in conflict with bosses as well as coworkers. These are distinct types of conflict as the power dynamic in each relationship is different: the boss can fire the employee, whereas coworkers (on equal level) cannot fire each other. Since conflict management is a context-dependent skill set, listening to exact responses to your questions will reveal a lot about how a person will work with you and others. Again, listen (and write down) the exact words used when responding to your questions.

I caution business owners to also remember that an interview is a sales pitch for the candidate. Candidates will aggressively sell themselves. Be careful to just ask your questions, then actively listen to the responses. If you're doing all the talking, active listening is not at play. I also caution business owners to provide limited information to the candidate about the company and the role for which they are applying. Many times, we want to make the candidate feel more comfortable, so we will over-share about what we are looking for, the position being filled, and even company details. You do not yet know these candidates well enough to share information about the company and the role unless expressly asked by the candidate. There will be time during the second and third interviews to share more about the company.

BEST OF BETH'S BLOG

··

Do You Hear What I Hear?

Over the Thanksgiving holiday, my daughter and I were listening to the radio. A song came on that we both love. I began belting out the tune at the top of my lungs and sang along to the chorus of the Zac Brown Band song. I sang "Long Gone," along in perfect pitch (to me at least).

My kid laughed uproariously. "*Mom*," she yelled, "Those aren't the words!"

I said, "Yes they are!"

She giggled. "No, really. It's not 'Long Gone'. It's 'Home Grown'!"

She had to Google it for me to believe her.

This misunderstanding happens in interviews for new employees all the time. Someone on the interview team will recount what the candidate said and someone else will have heard the words from the person completely differently. The very first step in the analysis of an interview for the hiring team is to agree to what the candidate actually said. The candidate's actual words are very important. For example, "My boss is really great to work with." Did the candidate really say "with?" Are you sure he or she didn't say "My boss is really great to work *for?*" That simple word changes the entire meaning of the sentence as well as the intent of the comment. The word "with" denotes that the candidate doesn't acknowledge the boss's authority, and if that's the case in the interview, what about when he or she has direct deposit?

I talk about listening to the exact words all the time to my clients to ensure they get to hire someone who will fit with the company culture, leadership style, and even the position itself. If you are not paying attention, you can miss something really important in an interview which can lead to a bad hire.

You can also really embarrass yourself in front of your teenage daughter.

•••

Nerves Happen

Nervousness is usually a good indication that the person really wants the job. It may be their habitual response to uncertainty, or they may be about to lose their house and need work badly. As the interviewer, you are just in the middle of an average busy day, so how do you help the candidate relax a little without defaulting to coffee-chat mode?

You can't stop candidates from being nervous. You can put them at ease, however, by first setting the agenda at the beginning of the interview. Say the interview will be about fifteen minutes; you will ask a series of questions and give the candidate the opportunity to do the same. Then at the end of the interview, you'll tell the candidate when to expect an answer from you.

Every candidate will say "thank you"—and visibly (or audibly) relax. The information reassures them by giving them a schedule to follow during the interview. "Okay," they think, "I do not have to guess about how to proceed with this interview and my interaction with this company."

This protocol speaks to the integrity of the interview and the company as a whole. Remember that you are marketing your company whenever you go out to the public. Once you have completed your first interview, let the candidate know what will happen next in your process. Here is an example of how to respond: "Steve, you will have an answer from us by Friday at 5:00. Either I will send you an e-mail letting you know that we're moving on with other candidates, or I will call you and get you scheduled for the second interview, but one way or the other, you will have an answer from us by Friday at 5:00." A professional, respectful protocol will put you in a rare minority of companies.

Phone Interviews

Depending on the client and the candidate, a phone interview may be more strategic or convenient than a face-to-face interview. Is a phone interview as effective? It depends. Over the phone, you do not get to assess the candidate with all your senses. Looking a candidate in the eye, feeling the strength of a handshake, and observing how a person physically interacts with his or her environment may provide you with meaningful indicators of a candidate's suitability. When you're communicating only by phone, you are reliant on only what you hear. With today's technology, consider video conference at a minimum, as the opportunity to observe a candidate on multiple fronts is ideal.

Nailing It

The people who "nail" the first interview share some basic traits:

- He appears accommodating: "I can start whenever you're ready."

- She's already had a conversation with their employer: "My current boss knows I'm looking." She's leaving on good terms with their bosses and coworkers.

- He knows exactly what he's looking for in his next position.

- She answers the preliminary and screening questions fully and completely.

- He comes prepared with questions, having done his research and envisioned himself in the role.

A candidate who nails the first interview won't necessarily nail the second or third one. The three interviews have distinctly different focuses, and are designed to uncover specific shortcomings and/or strengths of a candidate.

Next Steps

After all first interviews are conducted, review the interview responses, notify candidates who will not be returning of your intentions to continue the search, and select which candidates you would like to see again. If there are none, begin the process again by placing your job ad, screening candidates and conducting first interviews until you have found candidates you are truly interested in speaking to in more depth.

To move a candidates to the second interview, contact them and invite them back for the second interview. Include the full job description with your invitation. Ask the candidates to read the job description and come prepared with any questions about the job for the second interview.

You will also give candidates a short homework assignment for which they must present their solution to an actual issue they would face in this role. This is quite an effective filter of your candidates' technical suitability, as the assignment will reflect aspects of your industry or company. Try to provide homework assignments that will relate to a typical deliverable or accountability of the role.

CLIENT WISDOM

"This part of the process can seem harsh—it takes some getting used to. However, it is surprising how often it indicates how well the person will perform. It is shockingly accurate. It is screening, not elimination. There are little hints that come out, and I can't tell you how often people screw it up."

— Rick Taylor, President, Lefever Building Systems

For example, estimating costs can be in the required skill set for C-level executives in the construction industry. An effective assignment would be numbers-related and address, say, fleet management issues: How do you know when to lease versus buy? The candidate's plan should meaningfully illuminate technical intelligence.

Another example may be related to a problem your company is attempting to solve. During one of my searches, the client and I were looking for an executive director for a nonprofit. We had the top finalists prepare a marketing plan to develop the volunteer-management program and a brief outline of a fundraising program. We didn't supply them enough details to be able to create complete programs, but we did provide them with enough information to complete an assignment that would show us how they view fundraising versus volunteer management. We wanted to evaluate their *process*.

Put a time limit of one to three hours on the homework as respect to the candidate's time. Provide a homework assignment that is a serious evaluation tool that covers technical proficiency and industry knowledge, however, as well as his or her ability to follow directions, make a presentation, and stay on a schedule—real-world aspects of any job.

Now we move forward to the second interview, where we assess the skills the candidate brings to the table and how the skills match with the job description and duties of the role for which we are hiring. Make sure that you interview your "yesses" and your "maybes." This is the time to eliminate *only* your absolute "nos."

BEST OF BETH'S BLOG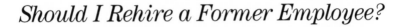

Should I Rehire a Former Employee?

People may leave your organization for any number of reasons: more money, a fresh opportunity, and loss of passion for a position are common. When a client asks for my opinion about rehiring a former employee, my honest answer is, "Well, it depends." Rehiring a former employee has advantages: training and ramp-up speed are often reduced. But the obvious disadvantage is wasting valuable resources on someone who isn't authentically committed to your business or you. These guidelines can help your decision-making process:

1. Did your rehire "leave well" by giving you notice and wrapping up projects before his or her departure? Did he or she leave on good terms and help with creating a job description or training a replacement? The manner in which your employee left you the first time will be the way he or she leaves you the second time.

2. Will your rehire add value to your current culture? What has changed since the last period of employment with you? Make sure this person is still a fit for your business and the position.

3. Realize that the rehire's tenure may be short-term. Your rehire likely left the first time because certain needs were not met. Will you be able to meet those needs now? Make sure that you address those unmet needs before bringing this person back on board.

One of my former colleagues in the restaurant industry regularly had kitchen staff who would periodically leave for more money, fewer hours, etc. He always thanked them for their service and let them pursue the new opportunity. Invariably, they would realize that life was not always greener on the other side of the fence and ask to come back. The ones who left with integrity were hired back immediately. Those who left ungracefully were not hired back.

···

CLIENT WISDOM

"You can see how quick they think on their feet. And how they match against exactly what we are looking for."

— Rhiannon Cochran, co-owner, Dream Dinners

"I think a lot of candidates expect to talk about their skills, so they are surprised by the scenario questions. The key is this: you can develop a skill set. How they intuitively handle situations is hard to teach but imperative to know."

— Anonymous

"The scenario-based questions placed the candidate in a 'what if' situation, and then I knew how they would come across to my clients. I also learned what training would be required and how they will fit with my team."

— Lisa Haas, Founder and President, Actuate Social

"This is where you learn if they told the truth on their resume. Do they really have the skills that they said they did?"

— Sean Lind, co-owner, Illuminations by Design

"This is the 'truth' meter. I could tell if people were telling me the truth. Did they pause, consider the question? I could see consistency or lack thereof in how answers were given. People weeded themselves out."

— Steve Caldara, President, Caldara, Wunder, and Associates

"This interview is for figuring out if the candidate is a good fit from our company's perspective."

— Matt Mendez, Founder and President, SpinFusion

CHAPTER 6

....

Step Six: Can This Person Do the Job?

The first interview has provided global insights into your candidates' work ethic, management requirements and cultural fit; the second interview will give perspective on what the new employees can offer your company, should they be hired. This interview is often an hour in length and should be expansive to determine true ability to perform the duties of the role.

Now is your chance to ask your candidates the honed list of questions regarding the technical aspects of the job. However, before we get too deep into the second interview process, let's discuss a screening point that comes up between interviews one and two: Asking your candidates to complete a homework assignment. Often, the concept of providing homework and requesting a presentation can be very insightful into your candidates' potential as your new hires. Be prepared, though—there are people who will come who haven't done the homework and who will come prepared to bypass this portion of the interview process. There was even one guy who brought his wife instead of his homework assignment. "To help answer any questions," he said. Seriously?

Remember the woman with the job description highlighted in pink? She said, "These are the things that I won't do for you."

We responded with, "Thank you very much for letting us know that before we hired you. Thank you so much for your time, we wish you success in your efforts." And we parted ways.

The point is that candidates often will consider the homework assignment and the job description as negotiable; they'll come in with edits, exemptions, side projects, even new duties. A job is not dictated by a candidate; a job is a set of duties and outcomes defined by

©Glasbergen
glasbergen.com

"Did you notice I called myself an *applican,* not an *applican't* ?"

you that propel the company to the next level. Your focus is on the needs and vision for the company; hence, the role you've described is what you are hiring for. Anything less (or more) will not serve you, regardless of what a candidate may appear or agree to contribute.

Upon calling one strong candidate following the first interview, I told him, "I'm pleased to tell you we're asking you to come and present to us some of your analytical skills, so I have this homework assignment for you." And he said, "Well, if it's not too much homework, because really I'm above that." He told me, "I left school a long time ago and I don't need to do that anymore."

Okay, he's obviously not interested. "Thank you very much for letting me know," I told him. "We will move on with other candidates." From the business owner's perspective, this sort of reply reveals a variety of dynamics that would come up in the workplace: the need to provide the boss with material being requested, the mindset around doing certain projects (or *gasp*! learning!), arrogance

CLIENT WISDOM

"Our Board had a very poor track record with hiring. The scenario questions gave the candidate a chance to act versus react, and that's the way to build a team."

— James May, Board President, Doss Heritage and Culture Center; Vice President, First Financial Bank (retired)

regarding self-image, and more.

I once interviewed a man who whipped out a switch blade to slice open a FedEx envelope that contained his references. I feared for my safety and the safety of my clients, so I gracefully ended our session by very politely thanking him for the interview and for his time and references. Whether he meant to scare us or not doesn't matter. He did. He was not hired.

And yet another example of a response to homework reveals a somewhat passive-aggressive and, again, self-important trait. With instructions to provide analysis about a project, I gave a candidate these caveats: "Please complete this assignment in one to three hours. We're not looking for you to solve the world's problems. We're looking to see your process and how you might think about this, from a big-picture standpoint."

The candidate came in and his homework was beautiful. However, he'd spent *eight* hours on it and he made sure that we knew that he spent eight hours on it.

What the "extra effort made" really meant was that he didn't

CLIENT WISDOM

"It doesn't matter if they get the right answer; it matters how much effort they put into their presentation and what questions they ask us."

— Roger Crawford, MEP Engineering

follow the directions set forth. That's not going to work for our ideal employee either. Why would such extra effort not be considered a plus? Because you can imagine, in the real world, we wouldn't necessarily have all day for him to work on this. He implied he resented that we were not appreciative of all the time he put into the project, when that was not what the parameters had been. He expressed that he could, of course, provide great material if given an appropriate amount of time to complete the project, yet since we had stated one to three hours, he assumed we were trying to set him up to fail.

He didn't see that he had re-invented the evaluation criteria. He wanted to be evaluated on the eight hours of work that he did, not whether he followed our directions. He could have just said, "I want you to evaluate me on what I choose to do, not what you ask me to do."

Now, it would have been a totally different scenario if he had called me and said, "I'd really like to spend some more time on it. Is that allowable?" In this case, the job was for an

CLIENT WISDOM

"The homework conveys more than anything else how badly the candidate wants this job. We see who bothers to prepare. Who took it seriously? I'd never done that before. And frankly, the people with the best homework are the ones that we hire."

— Rick Taylor, President, Lefever Building Systems

engineering firm that charges very expensive hourly rates. If I tell you one to three hours and you spend eight, you've just blown my labor cost. Requesting more time rather than assuming it shows much more awareness and respect for the concerns and responsibilities of the supervisor and the company; it demonstrates thinking from a management level. You would be glad this person is thinking big-picture and is company-goals motivated.

Skills Do Matter—Sort Of

You may have expected skills assessment to be the most critical part of the second interview process. You're thinking, "Sure, Beth, my candidates are available, seem nice, leave their knives at home—but do they have the skills? That's all I want to know."

Recognize that there are a few ways to demonstrate skills—and confident, talented (or desperate) candidates can *tell* you all about their skills. Let me share with you how this concept of assigning homework came about.

BEST OF BETH

Example Questions for the Second Interview:

- *Tell me about a time when you managed your time.*

- *Tell me about a time when you were overwhelmed.*

- *Tell me about a time when you set up a system.*

One of my clients wanted to hire a particular woman, and I really, seriously, did not want him to hire this person. I adore him and he adores me, and we are very good business colleagues, but it unnerved me that I could not convince him that she was a very bad fit. As a compromise, I said, "Let's have her do a homework assignment. Let's have her present to us," because presentations skills were a big part of the position. He agreed.

Well, she came in and blew it. The homework had wet spots all over it (she'd dropped it in the snow), and a corner was ripped off. And not only was the presentation not good, but the content was poorly done and full of typos. He did not hire her. (The person he did hire, using the *Response Analysis System*, has been there for over five years.)

The homework assignment allows you to evaluate not only the candidate's presentation skills but their foresight and attitude. I'm shocked at how many amazing C-level people will arrive for the second interview and say, "My printer broke down this morning," or "I'm sorry, I ran out of black ink," or "I only brought one copy," even though they know that multiple people will be sitting at the interview table. Or, worse, "I didn't print it out at all. Don't you have it? I emailed it to you". Someone who has passion for a particular job will exhibit self-agency, full accountability, and meticulous preparation.

BEST OF BETH'S BLOG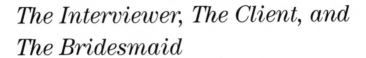

The Interviewer, The Client, and The Bridesmaid

Several weeks ago, my client and I called a candidate to get her scheduled for an interview. She asked for a phone interview at noon on the Friday afternoon that we had available for interviewing. She was very specific about the time. When I asked her if there was a reason for that particular time, she responded by saying, "Yes. I am in a wedding that day and it starts at 2:00." Since we schedule phone interviews all the time, I asked her if another day and time might be better, and she said, "No. I do *not* want to miss out on this opportunity."

On the day of her interview, I asked her if she was ready for the wedding, and she said "Yes. We have done our hair and makeup, and I am sitting in a church pew in my bridesmaid's dress. This is a first for me." It was a first for me and the client as well.

The most amazing part about that interview wasn't the dress or dedication to taking the call, although these were great steps to showing her enthusiasm for the position; it was actually in her preparation. She had done thorough research on the company. She referred to Yelp reviews. She asked excellent questions and she referred to her list of questions several times. She knocked the ball out of the park—all in her bridesmaid dress.

Brilliant. Truly brilliant.

••

"Both job candidates are equally educated, equally experienced and equally qualified, but one can play *Layla* on his armpit!"

The homework assignment is also a great arbiter when more than one person is evaluating the candidates, and especially if anyone on the hiring team knows one of the candidates. The homework assignment takes subjectivity and personal bias out of the equation.

As with the homework assignment, the questions in the second interview need to be actual technical scenarios. There are two reasons for this. First, you educate the candidate about the challenges of the position. Second, you get a feeling for how intuitively he or she will handle those and similar challenges.

The questions will reveal what the candidate knows and doesn't know about how to perform these future duties. Even if the candidate has relevant industry and job experience (remember the Myth of the Top 5), you or one of your staff must teach the new hire how a given skill and activity is performed and managed at *your* company. Essentially, this process determines the new hire's training program.

In addition, by asking questions around the technical aspects of the job via scenarios related to typical real-world projects and customers, you're not overselling the job. You're giving the candidate a heads-up about situations that come up—situations that, frankly, aren't fun or easy. It's a good-faith way to manage expectations and inform the person of the reality of the role. Candidates are more satisfied if they have a clear understanding of what their job is *before* they accept the offer.

An example of a scenario question you might ask is, "If you have three deadlines on Friday and know you're not going to get all of the work done, what do you do?" Such a question reveals if the candidate can self-manage so that you don't have to micromanage. Listen to word choice and tone, read body language, and observe the candidate's immediate reaction to the scenario.

While the second interview questions should be tailored to the challenges specific for the position you are hiring for, here are some examples to work from as you develop your own questions:

CLIENT WISDOM

"You are giving the candidate a sense of the workplace. You have to be honest about the good, the bad, and the ugly. Then you can attract the people who are a good fit. This is eye-opening for people who don't have experience but have great intuition and can do the job. Experienced people are on autopilot."

— Dan Schachtner, Denver Station Owner, XPO Logistics- Global Forwarding

- How do you approach learning something new?

- You have a tight deadline. You have a question but can't reach your supervisor. How do you proceed?

- You disagree with your boss. How do you proceed?

- You are beginning to become overwhelmed with your workload and feeling pressured and stressed. How do you react?

- You see a task that needs to be accomplished that is not within your job description. How do you proceed?

A client and I presented the following scenario to a candidate: "We have some vendors who are just not nice to some of the employees here. Your staff must be a little bit thick-skinned when dealing with this group. How will you manage?" The candidate answered, "People aren't nice for a variety of reasons. Often, it is not personal. My being nice to them will invite reciprocity in that moment. A little empathy goes a long way. I would respond with 'Gosh, it sounds like you've having a really bad day.'" (We hired that candidate.)

Another candidate was hired into a C-level position in a big construction company after completing the homework assignment. He arrived for his second interview with a beautiful presentation notebook for each member of the hiring team. He also e-mailed it ahead of time so that we could review it in advance. And he nailed the presentation.

Such committed, professional effort affirms the whole process, and it's phenomenal to witness.

In the second interview, the difference between a good and a poor impression is how intentionally and clearly the candidates present their skills to the hiring team. We *want* the candidates to succeed. We *want* to hire someone for the position. If the candidates make it easy for us to see their skill sets, then it's easy for us to hire them. I invite you to go deeper and look for a candidates who perceive and intuitively follow what makes it easy for you to accomplish your goals; observe how they think and make decisions and execute their actions before the hiring decision.

The second interview is an important indicator of a candidate's desire for the position. The determined candidate thinks, "I really want this job, so I'm going to do *X*, *Y*, and *Z* to make sure I get it."

BEST OF BETH

"Good employees are always good people—but good people are not always good employees."

If the candidate's completed homework and answers to the scenario questions of the second interview are still hitting on all cylinders, your follow-up correspondence will be an invitation to a third interview.

Get ready to assess *true* passion for the job.

CLIENT WISDOM

"The truth comes out in the third interview. Then, you compare that to the first interview. It's amazing!"

— Rhiannon Cochran, co-owner, Dream Dinners

"This interview is for figuring out if the job is a good fit for what the candidate wants. This is my favorite interview. It is incredibly powerful. It is a consistency check. I love that!"

— Matt Mendez, Founder and President, SpinFusion

"This is my favorite. I love it! You find out what motivates them, what inspires them. I have had people that I was rooting for that totally blew it. It allows the spirit of the individual to be seen. I know what I am getting, and I can lead my team."

— Lisa Harris, 23-year marketing veteran

"Their real core comes out. The cream rises to the top in the third interview and we hardly said anything! Amazing."

–Eric Burkgren, Branch Manager, Academy Mortgage

"We have seen far more people kick themselves out of the process than any other interview. For whatever reason, this process gets people to be very candid, and it is an eye opener."

— Rick Taylor: President, Lefever Building Systems

"I am a big believer in passion and vision. I love how they reiterate the job description- the person that thrives in this; you know you have made a good decision."

— Alan Wyngarden, President, Applewood Our House

CHAPTER 7

· ·

Step Seven: Is This Person Passionate about This Job?

The last interview in the *Response Analysis System* is designed to measure the candidate's passion for the position—an indicator that he or she will be around for the long haul. If passion is missing, this person is not the right employee for you or your business.

Sometimes a great candidate will say in the third interview, "You know, I don't like the answer I gave you to one of the questions in the last interview. I've been thinking about it, and here's what I'd like to say instead." Someone who is thinking about the job on off-time, reflecting on his or her previous presentation, and correcting any perceived misfires demonstrates motivation, humility, and initiative. This is what makes an A-list candidate and a top-notch hire.

The top reason for hiring people who are really excited about a job is that they are easier to train, less difficult, and more creative in their problem-solving. They're eager to learn new techniques, and challenges do not daunt them. They are yes-I-can and yes-I-will people, tapping into a seemingly unlimited store of energy. Respectful of their bosses and coworkers, they resolve conflicts promptly and professionally. They think about the company's goals in their off-time, and they can even be the employees who come up with crazy ideas that work. They often get the people around them excited and inspired.

For the last interview, you're searching for these characteristics. Will the job bring out the best in the candidates? Is it the job that really trips their trigger? Will your job make them happy?

For example, I asked a candidate I was interviewing for an Internet researcher position for a software development company, "If you could have any job in the world, what would it be?"

CLIENT WISDOM

"Thank God *for the third interview! It is 'make it or break it.' We have been ready to hire someone multiple times, and they have come into the third interview and blown it.*"

— Jon and Coralyn Wall, co-owners, Gonstead Family Chiropractic

"Oh, I'd be Madonna," he said. Having experienced him in the previous interviews, I was certain he'd be amazing at a job that requires performing live and entertaining a bunch of people.

But the job that we were hiring for—headphones on, in front of a computer, with no human interaction, forty to fifty hours a week—was never going to work for him energetically. He would've been at the water cooler entertaining his coworkers because he needs that human interaction, an audience to react to and adapt to. That's the kind of setting that energizes him, while we needed someone who derives energy from being alone. That was not going to be a good fit.

BEST OF BETH

"Passion trumps fear. If you can tap into their passion, and this is the job for them, they get animated and excited, and they can't wait to present to you. Passion trumps fear, always."

BEST OF BETH'S BLOG

Cry, Pull Your Hair Out, Laugh, Repeat

Last week, I placed a great employee in the right job with a great company, and everyone is really excited.

We all remember those moments in the interview process when we wanted to pull our hair out. Candidates just don't show up. The candidate looks right at you and says, "Wow, I don't like doing that type of work." (True story.) The potential employee shows up late with no apology or excuse and then proceeds to interrupt you for the entire interview. *Ugh!*

I have had days where I just wanted to bang my head against the interview table over and over and over again.

And then? When you least expect it—when you think that you will *never* find the right person *ever*—your dream candidate walks through the door. The candidate is on time, brings extra copies of resumes, references, and homework. He or she has done the right research, asks great questions and brings solutions, and then ends the interview by telling you that this is his or her dream job. The candidate makes it through the entire process and loves the offer.

And the kicker? The candidate can start on Monday.

Every single time I begin an interview process I know I am in for a roller coaster ride. I am going to laugh, cry, pull my hair out, bang my head on the table. But then I am going to laugh because I'm so happy for my clients and the candidate that they have found. I feel proud because we got through the process and it is the right fit for all. Then, I am going to shed a little tear, because the job is over. It is time for me to leave and go work with others, and the process starts all over again. *Sniff.*

Here in Colorado, I regularly interview candidates for management positions who say that their ideal job would be a ski instructor. Spending all day outside, on the snowy mountains, is fantastic. But I'm asking them to spend all day, every day, inside a building, managing people. That's a disconnect from the position and the person's happiness. That's not going to work.

What I want to say to such candidates is this: Go do that for a year. If that's something you really want to do, go follow your dream, follow your passion—and you might be surprised by the trajectory that launches as a result. An executive I met from Wells Fargo bank decided after 9/11 that he wanted to follow his dream of being a firefighter. He and his wife downsized their house and their expenses and, last I heard, he's doing the job he'd always dreamed of—firefighting. Now that's passion! Another candidate who was applying for a senior-level engineering position told me that his dream job would be a ballroom dance instructor on a cruise ship. I wanted to tell him to go do it. Life is short. His eyes lit up when he talked about dancing, but his eyes didn't light up when he talked about engineering. We didn't hire him.

By the time you get to the third interview, you've weeded out most of the bad-fit candidates. But that doesn't mean your short-list candidates won't show up in ways that disqualified others in the first and second interviews. The closer they are to getting the job, the more nonchalant or anxious they may get—nonchalant in that their overconfidence reveals an unsuitable aspect of personality or motivation; anxious in that they'll reveal additional information that may give insight into lack of suitability for the position.

> ## CLIENT WISDOM
> ....
> *"This gives them a moment of self-reflection. I get to find out what motivates them...what gets their juices flowing."*
> — Anonymous

The nonchalant candidate underprepares; the anxious candidate overthinks what he or she imagines you want to hear. The presence of true passion is what sets the finalists apart. The truly passionate candidates are consistent and clear about what they want to do and how this role serves their visions for their lives. That match between a candidate's motives and skills and your company's job description and vision is the magic. And it's possible, I promise you.

Now, just because it is possible to find a passionate, dedicated employee, it may not always happen immediately. I often let clients go all the way through to the third interview just for the practice, knowing we may need to start over. On the other hand, having done thousands of interviews, rarely have I predicted who ultimately gets the job offer after the first and second interviews. It seems that every time I have said to myself before the third interview,

"I've found the person," I've been wrong. Likewise, I have been equally surprised when I've gone into the third interview thinking we just aren't going to find the right match and the candidate hits it out of the park. The third interview can be that powerful.

The irony of the *Response Analysis System* is that your rigorous, up-front effort is so effective that it may not result in a new hire on the first try. It is not uncommon to post two or three times for a position. However, during the process, the responses from candidates will help you refine your job description and job ad.

Again, the questions are not the critical component to the third interview. Instead, focus on the responses from the candidates. Typical questions I have asked have been:

- If you had no economic or practical considerations and you could have any job you wanted, what would it be?
- What was the best job that you have ever had, and why?
- What qualities do you believe limit you from reaching your potential?
- Name one event that frustrated your career growth?
- What kind of people do you find most difficult to work with?

- What kind of people do you work best with?

- What changes have you made in your approach to others in order to become more accepted in your work environment?

- Describe your understanding of this job.

Bottom line: In the third interview, you'll hear if the candidates really want *this* job through their responses about how they see themselves working *in the job*. Responses may include ideas for how to solve problems, streamline processes, and make themselves successful in the job. Great matches will describe your work environment and how they enjoy working in it successfully. These are the people you're ultimately looking for. For example, a great hire for an administrative-assistant role confessed during the third interview, "I love being counted on. I want people to depend on me for help." You're looking for someone whose deepest drives and desires match your mission—and this is what the third interview is designed to reveal. If you focus on the language the candidates use, you'll make a good hiring decision based on a passionate individual.

Are You Excited? You Should Be!

When you make your final decision, you should feel like you won the lottery. You and your hiring team should be giving each other high-fives with relief and excitement about having found your new employee. When you have found "the one," it should make you want to cheer.

Also, be sure to share the details of your effort with your new hire once he or she has officially joined your team. For example, "Barney, we took applications from over two hundred people from twelve states, interviewed thirty-eight people from ten states, and put sixteen people from five states through the second interview. You were one of four people from two states who made it to the final interview, and *you* are the person we chose. We put in a lot of work to find you, we waited for you, and we are excited we found you. If you have issues or problems you can't solve on your own, come to us; we want you to succeed. We put a lot of money, time, and resources into this process, and we are so happy you're on your team. We cannot wait to get started." How much impact do you think you can expect from this person? Regarding the actual job offer details, refer to the job description and job ad for specific deliverables and expectations to present, along with pay and benefits details.

The *Response Analysis System* should guarantee that the hiring manager never thinks again, "Oh, I hope I made the right decision." Instead, this process will be, every time, a robust exercise in visionary clarity about what (and who) will best serve your company. Yes, hiring a person for your team can be this powerful.

But you're not done yet.

Now you must take some steps to ensure that the effort to find your A-list employee doesn't go to waste.

Time to train.

BEST OF BETH'S BLOG

···

Zombies in the Workplace

Do you walk into your office and see zombies disguised as employees? Those lifeless bodies that wander around thoughtlessly in packs? Have you ever thought about how they got that way?

New employees are always so excited to start their new jobs. I have heard many new hires talk about their first day on the job just like they talk about their first day of school, with excitement and a lot of awe. So how is it that years or even months into their employment with a company, they lose their passion for the job?

Because we suck the life out of them with too many constraints and not enough direction. We make it hard for them to do their jobs with petty rules. We don't spend enough time training our new people, and we really don't take the time to explain our expectations to them. All of a sudden, we have the lifeless body of a previously excited employee.

If you look around and see zombies on your staff, it is time to take stock of your interviewing process, your training program, and your employee handbook. If you are dictating when someone can go to the bathroom, you are running a daycare, not a professional office. It is time for a redo.

And if that doesn't work, try chocolate.

•••

CHAPTER 8

....

See it Through: Maximizing the Impact of Your New Employee

You're excited, relieved, and happy. You feel like you've won the lottery with your new employee. The research shows, however, that more than half of new hires quit within the first six months. So how are you going to avoid this critical pitfall?

They Won't Blow It—Unless You Do

Many new hires end up quitting (or, worse, get angry or indifferent, and stay) for these reasons:

- They weren't trained in company procedures

- They didn't receive specific skill training

- Nobody spent time with them

- They had to make up the job as they went along

- They weren't given feedback on their initial efforts

- They weren't clear about their supervisor's expectations

When the above happens, new hires feel confused, thrown to the wolves, and cracks immediately form in the rapport they were so sure they had established with their colleagues. They are quickly on a path to poor performance, a bad attitude, and all the issues that compelled you to read this book.

Some of my clients have said they'd be going out of town when their new hire starts. That's not okay. "Whoa, whoa, whoa," you may be saying. "I hire excellent candidates precisely because I need them to step right in and hit the ground running. I want them to go do what they do. Isn't that the point?"

No.

To leave somebody during their first ninety days with some version of "Figure it out for yourself" is *not* the way to build on the *Response Analysis System*. You cannot expect people to "hit the ground running," because every company, and every department in every company, is different. Ford and General Motors both make cars and

BEST OF BETH

"It is a myth that you can hire somebody today and they can 'hit the ground running' and be successful. They have to learn the players, the culture, what's currently working and not working. That's why training is crucial."

trucks, but they have different cultures, different internal priorities, and different systems. Being successful at Ford doesn't mean one can simply step into GM and be instantly connected, aware, efficient, and productive.

Leaving a new employee is rude, unprofessional, and truly naïve on your part. I've seen a new hire be left without a computer, a phone, significant contact with colleagues, and a place to sit, let alone an office or a desk. They weren't told where to park, which door to enter, or where the bathroom was located. This is not how you welcome a new member to your team.

I've had hiring managers say, "I'll invest more time in them if they're still here in ninety days." That just doesn't work: by then, the new hire has been in the trenches, figuring out the urgent priorities and making the job work on their terms as best they can. If you come back later and say, "I don't like how you're doing X, Y, and Z," the

> **CFO asks CEO "What happens if we invest in developing our people and then they leave us?"**
>
> **CEO: "What happens if we don't, and they stay?"**

new hire thinks, "Where were you when I needed help and guidance doing the things you hired me to do?" You have inadvertently created resentment. And if the first performance review after ninety days (or, heaven forbid, longer) is negative due to unclear expectations and poor resources, your new employee will start looking for another job. Not walking the talk you demonstrated during the interview process will feel like a bait-and-switch, creating uncertainty and distrust in your new hire.

How Not To Blow It

Spend as much time as you can with your new hires during the first ninety days. They're so excited, so optimistic— especially after being stressed out trying to find their perfect jobs. Now they can relax a bit and focus on their

©Glasbergen
glasbergen.com

"We're looking for someone who's capable of seeing the big picture."

new roles—those true to their core reasons for working.
They're as receptive as they'll ever be to your input and
directives.

Organizations make the following common failures and
skip these steps with the *Response Analysis System*.
Remember, this process isn't easy on the front end, but
you're aiming for long-term impact here.

The most skipped step is the thoughtful creation of the
Ideal Candidate Description (step 1 in chapter 2). This
effort prompts you to brainstorm a powerful vision for how
this role will help you achieve your company's mission. It's
one of the most productive ways you can work *on* your
business instead of *in* your business. If you don't do this,
you'll fill the position, yet again, without changing any of
its attributes and deliverables. Why should you expect
anything to change?

The second most-skipped step is the design and
implementation of a training program aligned with the
job description, and accounting for every hour of the
new hire's first two weeks. Start by introducing your new
employee to his or her office or workspace and providing
key items (e.g., welcome card, computer, phone, coffee
mug with your logo). Give your new hire a tour of your
facility, show any videos about your company's history, and
provide an overview of the position's tools and technical

equipment. A C-level employee should spend most of his or her time meeting people, exploring and asking lots of questions about how things work and what people precisely do in their roles. You may have seen the television show *Undercover Boss*: know that, during this time, the new hire may hear of inefficiencies, suggestions, gripes, and general nuances.

Just as the hiring process is an opportunity to market your company, a new hire's first ninety days are public-image-building opportunities. Think of how many people in the inner circle will be calling to ask, "So how was your first day?"

CLIENT WISDOM

"Beth, you are worth every penny we have paid you."

–Harold Kirschner, Certified Financial Planner, Sharkey, Howes & Javer

or "How's the new job going?" Your deliberate planning of the new hire's first two weeks will give him or her good reason to speak highly of your company. (Side note: The rise of social media means answers to those questions could be swirling out to dozens, hundreds, even thousands of people.)

Those first days and weeks will get things going on the right track or the wrong track. Put yourself in a new hire's shoes and make sure your actions align with all the words you've used to describe how you do things at your company. When you proactively invest in your new hire from the get-go, you launch a positive feedback loop that guarantees the person's equivalent investment and success. After two weeks of intense involvement, you can step back and check in at frequent intervals over the rest of the ninety-day period.

BEST OF BETH'S BLOG

··

Impacts of the Response Analysis System

A seasonal retail operation hired A-list Interviews to be in charge of hiring their temporary staff. I hired eight people, including the marketing director. The client reported these performance outcomes:

- 22 percent increase in revenue at Center #1

- 17 percent increase in revenue at Center #2

- 19 percent increase in customers

- 96 percent concurrent drop in customer complaints

- "I took vacations in the middle of my busiest time of the year with no problems. Time away for vacations was huge, and because of the decrease in problem calls throughout the days, I could enjoy the time off. I was able to take full days off without coming down on short notice to fill in or cover shifts."

Employee Comments:

- "Perfect. Great environment."

- "Staff members had same attitude—fun to be around."

- "I felt really comfortable and relaxed."

....

Another client sent out this e-mail at the end of 2016 after 17 hires:

Onward!

Your new hires will be a source of energy, ideas, and deliverables that will result in noticeable, if not profound, changes to your organization. These people will meaningfully contribute to your company culture, cultivate a happier environment, and add to your bottom line. Your vision of the workplace culture will manifest before your eyes as you hire more and more people via the *Response Analysis System.*

Consider that the effects of your smart hiring will last up to a year; beyond that time, macro forces in your industry, staffing and market changes, strategic goals, and the like will almost certainly change and influence your employee.

You must continually invest in the best practices of leadership, management, goal setting, team building, and incentives. Be sure to seek out the most up-to-date and relevant resources to maximize these important issues.

The title of this book is *Why Can't I Hire Good People?* I hope you've realized that you aren't looking for good people. You're looking for great employees—those whom you can work with (First Interview), who can do the job (Second Interview), and who are passionate about the job you're asking them to do (Third Interview). Employees who meet these three criteria generate, innovate, and move business to the next level. They are also better coworkers, better friends, better spouses and partners, better parents, and better children to their parents.

Focus on choosing good *employees*, and you will dramatically change the culture and success of your company.

The *Response Analysis System* will help you keep great people in the right positions so that your business can evolve into the amazing organization you've dreamed it could be.

RESOURCES AND FURTHER READING

Abrams, Rhonda M. *Hire Your First Employee: The Entrepreneur's Guide to Finding, Choosing and Leading Great People.* Palo Alto, CA: Planning Shop, 2010.

Boydell, Janet, Barry Deutsch, and Brad Remillard. *You're Not the Person I Hired!: A CEO's Survival Guide to Hiring Top Talent.* Bloomington, IN: AuthorHouse, 2005.

Fyock, Catherine D. *The Truth about Hiring the Best.* Upper Saddle River, NJ: Pearson Education/FT Press, 2008.

Gladwell, Malcolm. *Blink: The Power of Thinking without Thinking.* New York: Little, Brown and, 2005.

Harvard Business Essentials. "Harvard Business Review on Finding & Keeping the Best People." Harvard Business Review—Ideas and Advice for Leaders. Accessed January 19, 2017. https://hbr.org/product/baynote/an/10324-PDF-ENG.

Messmer, Max. *Human Resources Kit For Dummies, 3rd Edition.* John Wiley & Sons, 2012.

Michalowicz, Mike. *The Pumpkin Plan: A Simple Strategy to Grow a Remarkable Business in Any Field.* New York: Portfolio/Penguin, 2012.

Mornell, Pierre. *45 Effective Ways for Hiring Smart!: How to Predict Winners and Losers in the Incredibly Expensive People-reading Game.* Berkeley, CA: Ten Speed Press, 1998.

Plotkin, Robert. *Preventing Internal Theft: A Bar Owner's Guide.* Tucson, AZ: P.S.D. Pub., 1988.

Yate, Martin John. *Knock 'em Dead Hiring the Best: Proven Tactics for Successful Employee Selection.* Avon, MA: Adams Media, 2014.

A-list Interviews, Beth Smith: www.a-listinterviews.com

CLIENT WISDOM

"We always knew what we wanted, and now we have it—solid people who have our backs, and we in turn have theirs."
— Jim Eddy, Co-owner, Dream DinnersDinners

"They work together as a team better than ever before. Tenure is three to four times longer than it used to be."
— Carol Eddy, co-owner, Dream Dinners

"Our staff thought of this as voodoo at first. But now that two-thirds of them have been hired through this process, they view it as a rite of passage."
— Rick Taylor, President, Lefever Building Systems

"I know these candidates better than those in any interview process that I've done before"
— Karlton Childress, Certified Financial Planner, Sharkey, Howes & Javer

"We need to do our part to keep our new hires. The focus needs to be on retention. You have to stick to this process in order for it to work."
— Dan Schachtner, Denver Station Owner, XPO Logistics-Global Forwarding

"I don't worry. My employee has gone the extra mile every day for the last five years. He cares about what we do."
— Steve Caldara, President, Caldara, Wunder, and AAssociatesAssociates

ACKNOWLEDGMENTS

It takes a community to support a business, and I am eternally grateful for mine.

Here is my community, in alphabetical order:

A-list Interviews Advisory Board: Alan Wyngarden, Mark Heinritz, Rick Taylor, Roger Crawford, and Steve Caldara, you gentlemen are not only my clients, but my trusted advisors. You held my hand when I needed it and kicked my you-know-what when I needed that. All in all, I am a better business owner and a better person for knowing you.

A-list Interviews Clients: I have loved working with *all* of you. I learned so much. Thank you for your faith and trust.

Actuate Social: Lisa Haas, you took a relative unknown and made her an online expert. Wow! Lisa, you crawled through the trenches with me. Thank you.

Anita Turner Corwin: My friend who first read my book. She liked it! She really, really liked it!

Creative Exchange Marketing: Beth and Eric Boen: You single-handedly got me in front of the right people. My business took off because of you.

Harpo's: My home away from home. I haven't worked there in nine years, and still I am "Norm." Thanks, Mark and Charlie.

Indie Books International: This book was a figment of my imagination until I met Henry DeVries and his team. They brought my dream to light. Thank you!

Jane Jenkins: Upon hearing about my new business venture, you put me in front of one-hundred-ish business owners as the featured speaker. I am indebted to you.

Dr. Jon Wall, Coralyn Wall, and your staff: You quite literally helped me walk again. I don't know where I'd be without you!

Lynn Martin: CPA extraordinaire who keeps me and my books in line.

Mandi Hogan: My friend, marketing advisor, and all in all a beautiful woman.

Meryem Ersoz: We are on parallel paths always. I love that about us.

Marj Hahne: You had the guts to tell me that my first three drafts were, well, not so good. "There is a book in here, Beth. This isn't it." (You can't beat that coming from your editor.)

Matte Simmons: My friend, confidant, and financial advisor.

Sharon King and the Boulder SBDC: Thank you for giving me a place to practice, to learn, to grow, and to thrive.

Triple-D Girls: Laura Hein and Tina Ramey: Thanks for the mammaries…and the Cheez Whiz.

ABOUT THE AUTHOR

Beth Smith has been empowering business owners, hiring managers, and human resource directors for over a decade to interview and hire the right person the first time. She discovered the importance of the interviewing process when she made a poor hiring decision, which almost led to the demise of her first company.

After launching an enormous research project so that she could learn how to conduct more effective interviews, she concluded that there is a science to interviewing. She also discovered that many managers are thrown into the interview room, scrambling to figure out what to ask and what to listen for, instead of actually being taught how to conduct an effective interview. Beth's mission has become to transform the world through the interview process in order to promote happy and productive work environments for both employers and employees. To do this, she created A-list Interviews.

Through the research she did on the interview process and through the almost 20,000 candidates that she has interviewed, Beth developed the Response Analysis System. Studies done on the Response Analysis System show that 91 percent of those who were interviewed and then hired based on the Response Analysis System are still employed by the company twelve months later. The power of this system is from the advanced ability to listen to job applicants and measure their fit into an organization both culturally and for skill level.

Beth graduated from the University of Texas in 1995 with degrees in history and social work with a minor in English. She also studied psychology, philosophy, and child development. She has won several awards within her community and industry, such as, Women Who Make a Difference in Boulder, Business Owner of the Year, Certificates of Service for The Hill Alliance, and The Responsible Hospitality Group.

She currently lives in Boulder with her family. In her free time, Beth supports PawsCo, a Colorado animal rescue organization. She is also an avid swimmer, loves to lift weights, and is a die-hard football fan.